Navigating Your Career

More information about this edition and other books can be found at
www.boom.nl

© 2024 Sikko Onnes, Ron Soonieus, Remon Jasperse | Boom

Cover design: Studio Jan de Boer
Graphic design: Coco Bookmedia

ISBN   9789024458394
ISBN e-book 9789024458400
NUR   801

Sikko Onnes
Ron Soonieus
Remon Jasperse

NAVIGATING YOUR CAREER

A Young Professional's Guide to Why, How and Where You Want to Work

Boom

CONTENTS

INTRODUCTION

Of course I want to make an impact and do something with purpose... or is that just what everyone expects me to say? My friends all find start-ups cool... but do they really know what they're talking about? My family tells me to 'follow my passion'... but how can I, if I don't know what jobs are out there? And anyway, I'm not sure I've found my passion yet.

No wonder so many university leavers are paralysed by indecision, and so many young professionals find themselves in jobs they do not like. Why? Because there is a plethora of options. What's more, they are navigating the expectations of parents, friends and society, as well as their own desires – some of which may be unrealistic.

These dilemmas are the reason why we have written the book you hold in your hands, loosely based on the authors' highly rated course at the Business School of the University of Amsterdam. The chapters that follow address today's career challenges by offering new insights and tools to better understand yourself and the evolving job market. We critically examine generational characteristics and challenge the conventional wisdom of 'follow your passion'. We provide a comprehensive guide for those looking to tailor their career paths to their unique strengths and desires. We thoughtfully demonstrate how to match personal aspirations with the ever-shifting landscape of professional opportunities.

Additionally, the book offers a grounded overview on how the work environment has evolved into its current form, from the diverse generational viewpoints of the co-authors. This uniquely three-dimensional perspective provides aspiring young professionals with key insights that they would otherwise miss.

How are we going to achieve all that? First, our approach transcends the conventional model of climbing the career ladder and encourages a broader view of professional success. Quite apart from analysing your dilemma (and showing that it is perhaps not as bad as it seems), it addresses the crucial but rarely asked question: 'Why do you want to work?' Second, we include an online personality test (free of charge to purchasers of the book) that connects the many sectors, organisations and roles of the working world to your own natural preferences. Third, we present an overview of the three phases in working life, addressing how you can best realise your potential across the entirety of the career ahead of you. In particular, we explain the crucial transition from personal effectiveness to organisational effectiveness.

Just to make it clear, we will *not* identify your ideal career. Instead, we will equip you with the tools and methodology to find out for yourself what your first jobs might look like. These insights will help you to find the missing link between your preferences and the working world by developing a job market strategy.

Although this book is written mainly for undergraduates, recent graduates and early career changers, it also speaks to organisations seeking to recruit members of Generations Y and Z and parents seeking to better understand their children's career aspirations and challenges (as well as insights on how their own career has evolved). In addition, it will appeal to anyone interested in the job market, particularly professional recruitment consultants and careers advisers.

HOW TO USE THIS BOOK

We recommend reading the book in order because, together, the chapters present a strategic, structured approach to the job market. Having said that, some readers may prefer to skim through certain chapters or skip occasional sections. Here's a quick preview of all the chapters to help guide your reading.

CHAPTER 1: CONFRONTING YOUR CAREER

We live in a world with more opportunities than ever before. But in that case, why do so many people struggle to find personal and professional happiness? Why do so many twenty-somethings burn out? Why do so many others stall completely in their careers? And why do so few know what they want out of life? Welcome to the twenty-first-century phenomenon of the quarter-life crisis.

This initial chapter paints a picture of the quarter-life crisis and identifies the 'job-market dilemma' as the main source of the problem. Should you aspire to making money or societal impact? Should you seek prestige or intellectual satisfaction? Should you follow your passion or settle for a more practical option? The first step to resolving such dilemmas is to understand them.

CHAPTER 2: DISSECTING THE DILEMMA

The reasons for the job-market dilemma can be broken down into three distinct yet interrelated issues. First, there is a bewildering array of options available today, compared to even a few years ago. How can you possibly find out about all of them? Second, most of today's aspiring professionals are members of Generations Y and Z. Typically, the experiences of these two generations make it difficult for them to find their 'dream job', particularly when it comes to making trade-offs. Third, social media, peer and parental pressure are at an all-time high. How are you supposed to find your own path in life in the face of so many different influences and competing expectations?

This chapter takes a deep historical dive into each of three issues and reassures readers that they are not alone. It explains the evolution of the job market over time, the differences between the various generations (Silent, Boomers, X, Y, Z and A), as well as the major game changer since the beginning of this century: digitalisation. Finally, it lays the ground for focusing on why *you* — not your friends, your parents or your generational herd — want to work.

CHAPTER 3: WHY DO YOU WANT TO WORK?

It's strange how few people ask themselves the question in the title of this chapter. To put it simply, if you can't define what you're looking for, how on earth can you recognise it when you see it out there in the job market? Perhaps we shouldn't be surprised that in a world with more information than ever before, so many people make bad career decisions...

Based on experience and research, we have identified the seven most important reasons why people want to work. This chapter helps you to understand your personal reasons for working by unpacking them one by one. It's a good first step to becoming more intimately acquainted with yourself – in terms that relate to the job market.

CHAPTER 4: KNOW THYSELF

Personality tests – they always teach you something, right? They confirm your suspicions about yourself, they make you confront traits that you've never faced up to, and sometimes they tell you something entirely new about yourself! But the one thing they can't do is find you a perfect job. That requires further work...

This crucial chapter analyses how getting to know yourself better can help you find the perfect job... and how even an imperfect job can help you to understand yourself. The chapter also uncovers the sense and nonsense of personality and aptitude tests. Best of all, it introduces a work-focused assessment tool that we have been using for many years in our course for master's students. This powerful instrument, the AEM-Cube, gives insights into the kinds of roles and environments where you will naturally thrive, those where you will need to make more of an effort and those that you might want to avoid altogether.

CHAPTER 5: THE WORKING WORLD

How do you translate your personality and reasons for working into a sector, organisation or role, especially as you've never ventured into the world of work before? Of course, you can go to career events, talk to recruiters and recent recruits, even do internships and work experience, but these are essentially random encounters. Why should you leave such an important matter to chance?

This chapter tries to improve the reader's chances and broaden their scope by giving a systematic overview of what's out there. We start with a quick overview of *sectors* – from business to government to not-for-profit. Then we move on to a typology of *organisations* by size, ownership, culture and stage of development. Finally, we look at roles. What do all those opaque job titles mean and how do they all fit together?

CHAPTER 6: WHERE PERSONALITY PROFILES MEET JOB ROLES

Now you know yourself, and you understand the job market better than you did before. But you still have one major problem: how do you translate your personality profile into a role, an organisation and/or a sector?

In this chapter, we return to your personal AEM Cube profile (as introduced in Chapter 4) and start to map it onto the working world (as described in Chapter 5). We also tell you about other people's profiles, which should give you a head start in making the most of your first job and ease your progress through the subsequent phases of working life.

CHAPTER 7: THE THREE PHASES OF WORKING LIFE

In all honesty, you're probably focused on your first job. At the start of your career, it's normal not be too interested in the long term. We fully understand that. However, with so many options on the table, we recommend that you try to understand their future implications.

This chapter helps the reader to deal with the questions that arise once they start work. What is my potential? How can I ensure that I fulfil that potential? Where should I be heading? Who should I become: a specialist or a generalist? When should I make my first job move? To answer these questions, we use the simple yet effective metaphor of building a house. First, you must assemble your toolbox and learn how to use your tools. Second, you must design and build a house that fully meets your personal needs. Third, you can settle down and live in the house you have constructed, continuing to make the improvements that will make it your home. Each of these career phases requires a different approach. To help you choose the right approach at every stage, we carried out some original empirical research, which offers some interesting takeaways about career strategising.

CHAPTER 8: HOW TO CHOOSE

This career business sure seems complicated! You have to recognise the dilemma, understand your personality, uncover your innermost desires, scan the entire world of work and project yourself into the future. How on earth can you do all of this at once?

This chapter brings together all the considerations of the previous chapters, using the model of the search engine. The reader now has a worldwide web of possibilities *and* the correct search terms. But realistically, the algorithm may not identify a job with everything they are looking for, let alone put the ideal career at the top of the list. Any job search inevitably involves trade-offs and compromises – and it helps if the job seeker can weigh them objectively.

This book is just a starting point for the reader's own research and information-gathering – over many cups of coffee, both alone and with other people. This final chapter deals with the practicalities of that process, whether for a first job, an early move or a later career change. It takes you back to the starting point, and the questions to ask yourself along the way. It reemphasises the importance of navigating a strategic course with an open mind, looking beyond the usual suspects for the role that really resolves your own job-market dilemma.

www.navigatingyourcareer.info

CHAPTER 1
CONFRONTING YOUR CAREER

At university in the Netherlands, Remon dedicated himself to achieving high grades, securing competitive internships, gaining international experience and actively participating in student clubs. The goal was clear – to compile the 'perfect CV'. His resumé, he thought, would act as the golden key after graduation, unlocking opportunities with top-tier companies, guaranteeing a substantial salary and propelling his career into a higher gear.

As Remon meticulously built his resumé, ticking off achievements throughout his university years, he felt a surge of accomplishment and invincibility. However, as he neared the completion of his master's at a reputable university in China – the final item on his to-do list – a wave of doubts swept over him. In his relentless pursuit of the perfect CV, he had lost sight of a crucial question: what did he truly want? Beyond having a vague idea of landing a highly paid job, gaining expertise and making an impact, Remon lacked a clear understanding of his genuine desires, let alone the kind of organisation that might satisfy those desires. The quest for an impressive list of achievements had overshadowed the exploration of his aspirations and goals.

Remon, as you've probably guessed, is one of the authors of this book. In fact, the book was inspired by the 'job-market dilemma' that he was experiencing just a few years ago – and which his two co-authors helped to resolve. The three of them have now joined forces to help other students, recent graduates and young professionals who are contemplating their future careers and find themselves in a bewildering maze of possibilities. Of course, not everyone is like Remon. Different people from different cultures experience the same dilemma in a vast variety of ways. But the source of the problem is the same for everyone. We call it the 'job-market dilemma', part of a broader phenomenon called the 'quarter-life crisis', and we'll try to explain both concepts in this chapter. But first, let's meet Remon's friend, Olivia.

In contrast to Remon's proactive approach, Olivia didn't spend her undergraduate years meticulously planning and strategizing for her career. She took a more laid-back approach to her studies, focusing on passing courses and enjoying college life. Olivia didn't actively seek internships or international experiences during her academic journey. Unlike Remon, Olivia figured she could throw together a job application at the last minute.

On completing her education, Olivia came face to face with a stark reality. While her classmates seemed to have clear career goals and impressive resumés to match, she felt unprepared and uncertain about her next steps. She realised she hadn't given enough thought to her career during her studies and was now scrambling to figure out what she wanted to do with her degree. Unlike Remon, who had a moment of introspection near the end of his master's programme, Olivia's realisation came much later. Looking back, she wished she had invested more time and effort in exploring her passions and building relevant skills during her college years, rather than waiting until it was time to enter the workforce.

Though their realisations occurred at different times, Remon and Olivia both made the sudden discovery that they didn't understand the working world. They were unfamiliar with the differences between industries they weren't exposed to (e.g., healthcare versus energy), the varying skill sets required by different types of organisations (e.g., start-ups versus large organisations) and the potential long-term implications of their career choices (e.g., if they joined an NGO straight after university would it be impossible to get a job in a company – and vice versa).

Remon and Olivia were relieved to discover they weren't the only ones facing challenges. Many of their classmates were in the same boat. Some decided to change their academic trajectories, while others switched jobs (sometimes more than once) within a year of graduation. Everyone was having trouble moving from academia to the working world.

WELCOME TO THE WORLD OF WORK… AND THE JOB-MARKET DILEMMA

The *Harvard Business Review*[1] highlights the three main reasons why most graduates feel uncertain as they transition into work. First, when you enter the job market, *feedback* is not presented as clearly as in school. Instead of a syllabus and grades, you now face office politics and qualitative comments about your work, leaving room for potentially distressing ambiguity. In the past, your grades were the primary measure of your progress. Now, however, your supervisors, each with their own way of communicating and unspoken expectations, evaluate your performance, which can be confusing. Secondly, and relatedly, *relationships* take on a very different kind of role in the workplace. While sympathies and shared interests might have defined your circle of acquaintances at university, networking with people you don't necessarily like is essential for career advancement. Managing your professional self without exposing your private vulnerabilities is another challenge you probably didn't encounter while studying. Thirdly, there is a higher degree of *accountability* in the working world. Instead of passing exams and writing assignments for your own benefit, your performance now impacts others. Combined, these three factors can make adapting to the world of work much more distressing than you might have hoped.

While past generations of graduates faced similar challenges, they didn't have to contend with today's fast-changing job market. LinkedIn's analysis of career paths in 2016 reveals double the number of job changes compared to the early 2000s, with a quarter of employees switching roles in their first year. The once straightforward path from graduation to career success is now a complex maze. Rapid technological advancements, global industry shifts and ever-changing employer demands create further twists and turns in the labyrinth. It's a new – often intimidating and perplexing – world.

In navigating this evolving landscape, most people find a troubling mismatch between the knowledge they acquired in lecture halls and the understanding they need – both of themselves and of the working world – to find a fulfilling career. What they learned at school is disconnected from the realities of the modern workplace. This disparity gives rise to challenges that many graduates – maybe including you – grapple with as they endeavour to carve out a place for themselves in the professional world.

We use the term 'job-market dilemma' to encapsulate the multifaceted challenges and uncertainties that individuals, especially recent graduates, encounter at the start of their careers. This dilemma arises from a variety of factors that collectively shape the complex landscape those transitioning from education to the workforce must navigate – a landscape marked by economic shifts, evolving industry demands and the paradox of needing experience to gain experience. We will explore these factors in greater detail in Chapter 2.

Soon-to-be graduates often envision embarking on a fulfilling career in their chosen field as soon as they finish their academic journey. However, reality often falls short. Obstacles like fierce competition, limited opportunities and the paradoxical need for experience can make landing even an entry-level job daunting. A recent study of 7,500+ college students revealed that job market anxiety begins even before official entry, with 36% of those in their final year feeling unprepared for their career[2]. Based on our own experience, this figure likely underestimates the actual number.

Some college students (like Olivia) might not think about the working world during their education; others (like Remon) might be focused on building the perfect resumé. Either way they will be unprepared. They will need deep introspection, awareness of how the working world operates, knowledge of potential career paths and a variety of practical skills, if they are going to land that first 'dream job'. And even when they think their dream has come true, they will probably find that the job is nothing like they'd imagined.

Essentially, the 'job-market dilemma' is shorthand for the gulf between the optimistic expectation of an effortless transition from education to a rewarding career and the stark realities of a highly competitive and constantly shifting job-market landscape. Graduates must navigate these challenges actively. They must recognise the need for continuous learning, endless adaptability and a strategic approach, if they are to align their aspirations with the evolving demands of the professional world. The path from education to work is not straightforward but full of potholes and wrong turns, which demand resilience, planning, and a clear mental map of the modern employment landscape.

ZOOMING OUT TO THE QUARTER-LIFE CRISIS

As we resolve the job-market dilemma within these pages, it's also important to acknowledge its connection to a broader phenomenon commonly experienced in the years after graduation: the quarter-life crisis.

The quarter-life crisis is the period of uncertainty and anxiety that people often experience in their mid-20s to early 30s. It's marked by confusion, doubts, and a sense of being overwhelmed by life goals, career and personal identity. External pressures, such as societal expectations, financial concerns, peer-group comparisons, lack of a clear life plan, and the disparity between expectation and reality all contribute to the complexities of this period.

While the 'quarter-life crisis' may seem like just another excuse for the 'snowflake' generation (and while the *mid-life* crisis is more widely recognised), the concept deserves to be taken seriously. According to global research by LinkedIn[3], 75% of 25- to 33-year-olds have experienced a quarter-life crisis. See Exhibit 1.1 for an overview of its various interconnected elements.

Exhibit 1.1: Dimensions of the quarter-life crisis

Dimension	Description	Example
Identity Exploration	People of this age grapple with questions about who they are, what they value and where they see themselves in the larger context of life. This self-discovery extends beyond the surface, delving into personal values, passions and the alignment of these aspects with chosen career paths.	Ava, 23, feels suffocated in her corporate job in finance. Inspired by her love for animals, she quits her job and volunteers at a wildlife sanctuary. Through caring for injured animals and advocating for conservation, Ava discovers a deep sense of fulfilment and purpose she never found in the corporate world.
Career Anxiety	As graduates transition from the structured environment of academia to the professional world, they often face dilemmas about their chosen career paths. The pressure to find a fulfilling and meaningful job can be overwhelming, leading to anxiety about whether the chosen profession aligns with personal values and long-term goals.	Jack, 25, faces crippling anxiety after being laid off from his dream job at a tech start-up. Despite feeling defeated, he channels his frustration into launching his own app. Through relentless determination and countless sleepless nights, the app gains traction, leading to a lucrative acquisition offer that validates his skills and restores his confidence.
Future Uncertainty	Societal expectations weigh heavily on young professionals, pushing them to achieve financial independence, career success and stable relationships. The pressure to meet these milestones by a certain age contributes to a pervasive feeling of urgency and uncertainty.	Lin, in her mid-20s, feels the societal pressure to achieve financial stability. However, her passion lies in pursuing a creative career that might offer less financial security. Balancing her aspirations with societal expectations creates uncertainty about her future, making decisions about career and life milestones challenging.

Relationship Challenges	Recent graduates may re-evaluate existing relationships, question their compatibility with long-term goals or experience challenges in forming meaningful connections. Navigating the complexities of personal and romantic relationships becomes a significant aspect of this transitional period.	Dani and Nadia, both 26, face strain in their relationship due to competing career demands. Despite their love, they drift apart under the weight of work stress. They commit to regular date nights and open communication, reigniting their connection and reaffirming their commitment to each other.
Existential Reflection	Beyond the tangible aspects of identity and career, the quarter-life crisis often involves existential reflection. Individuals grapple with questions about the meaning and purpose of life, pondering the broader significance of their existence.	Elena, 24, faces existential questions after the sudden death of her best friend. Struggling to find meaning in her own life, she embarks on a soul-searching journey, volunteering at a homeless shelter and immersing herself in mindfulness. Through acts of kindness and introspection, Elena finds solace in helping others and discovers a newfound appreciation for the fragility of life.

An additional challenge of the quarter-life crisis is that 20- and 30-somethings feel under pressure to have fun! As a result, they (or those around them) may downplay the difficulties they face. The American Counselling Association (ACA)[4] highlights the importance of acknowledging the quarter-life crisis and cautions against the cultural assumption that the age 25 universally represents the peak of happiness and fulfilment.

The quarter-life crisis has gained greater attention recently because of the disturbing increase in burnout among Gen Z and millennials (there's more information about the definitions of these and other generations in the next chapter). According to the *Deloitte Global 2023 Gen Z and Millennial Survey*[5] of 22,000 employees across 44 countries, about 50%

of people from these generations report feeling stressed or anxious all or most of the time, with rates increasing. The pressure to succeed and make the 'right' decision about the future often involves thorough self-reflection, research and decision making, which can be emotionally and mentally draining. In addition, due to intense competition during their studies and early career, young professionals may feel forced to work too hard and strive for perfection.

All of these factors combined, together with the constant flood of information through social media feeds about peers' seemingly polished lives and careers, can lead to high levels of anxiety and fear of missing out. It is alarming that one in three young adults now report experiencing symptoms of common mental health problems, such as depression or anxiety disorder, compared with one in four in 2000[6]. Psychological well-being and career indecision are directly linked, whereas lower self-esteem and poor self-efficacy are associated with a high degree of career *in*decision. There is compelling evidence that the connection is causal and that it goes both ways, with career indecision affecting mental health and vice versa.

Of course, career indecision is, to some extent, a normal developmental challenge and only becomes cause for concern if it turns into chronic career *indecisiveness*. There may even be some upsides. Short-term stress regarding early career indecision can lead to better long-term career outcomes, especially if it motivates students to explore opportunities more thoroughly and encourages them to reflect more deeply on their own aspirations. On the one hand, acquiring more information on the industry or role you're interested in can't do any harm! On the other hand, a fear of commitment can gradually turn into drifting through life or, worse, paralysis. This book is designed to help you take your first steps into the workplace with confidence, by enabling you to learn about yourself, learn about the job market and learn how the two best fit together.

FROM FRESH GRADUATES TO CAREER CHANGERS

Understanding the quarter-life crisis is just the start of addressing your personal job-market dilemma, which may not be (like Remon and Olivia's) associated with the transition from university to work. Our advice throughout this book is equally relevant to readers contemplating an early-stage career change.

For almost every young professional, from the fresh graduate to the 30-something with a decade or more of experience, the job-market dilemma exists, transcending industries, cultures and for-profit and non-profit organisations. Here are just a few real-life examples that we've encountered:

- A creative professional seeking to transition into a corporate role;
- A doctor who, after discovering a preference for advising clients over hospital work, shifted into strategy consulting;
- A technology enthusiast who opted for a career with greater social impact, leaving a well-paid job;
- An environmentalist aiming to drive change from within one of the companies they once boycotted, by exploring roles in corporate sustainability;
- A young professional who, having initially joined a big company, discovered a better cultural fit in a start-up;
- A lawyer who left a prestigious job at a boutique legal firm to pursue a passion for gardening, eventually becoming a landscape architect.

These examples prove that strategic decision-making and adaptability can conquer the job-market dilemma, regardless of the professional arena.

Let's go a bit deeper into the story of one person we encountered – Yme – a business student who chose to pursue his passion for music.

Yme

After completing his secondary education in Europe and studying for one year at an American high school, Yme was at a crossroads, uncertain about his path forward. Influenced by his father and brothers, he initially chose to pursue an economics degree at the University of Rotterdam in the Netherlands. However, this choice proved to be a total mismatch, prompting a move to Amsterdam with similar results.

Amidst his uncertainty, Yme discovered a passion for electronic music and immersed himself in the vibrant international club and festival scene. A coincidental encounter with a female DJ led him to leave his studies. The decision didn't sit well with his father, who questioned his lack of a backup plan.

Determined to carve out a niche in the world of electronic music, Yme embarked on a zigzagging journey, taking on various roles – from waiter and burger flipper to recruitment agency staffer – to fund his dream of becoming a DJ. The challenges were numerous, and the onset of the pandemic further complicated his path. However, an unplanned opportunity with a fintech company shifted his perspective, revealing that he might have commercial skills that he could apply to his passion for electronic music.

As Yme honed his skills, he became involved in organising club events and booking DJs, steadily building a network and reputation in the industry. His perseverance and dedication eventually caught the attention of one of the world's largest festival organisers, leading to a role as a booker in Amsterdam and later in Barcelona.

Today, Yme stands confident and fulfilled, embracing his role as booker and DJ in an industry he understands and loves. His journey serves as a testament to his struggle but also to his perseverance and passion.

Another professional we worked with is Zack, who, despite being born in a city surrounded by wealth, decided to follow his passion for sustainability abroad.

Zack

Zack's story begins in Dubai, a city known for its dazzling skyscrapers and fast-paced, money-driven culture. After gaining his finance degree, he dived headfirst into the corporate consulting world, where his intelligence and dedication quickly propelled him up the corporate ladder. The financial rewards were substantial, but Zack started to feel a growing emptiness inside as the years went by.

The city's relentless pursuit of wealth left him questioning his values and priorities. He longed for a more fulfilling life that would connect him with a deeper purpose. That's when an unexpected opportunity knocked on his door – his consulting firm offered him the chance to relocate to Canada. Zack saw this as a lifeline, an opportunity to escape the materialistic culture of Dubai and get closer to nature.

Zack embraced the opportunity, and with a mix of excitement and trepidation, he packed his bags. Canada's natural beauty – pristine landscapes, lush forests and sparkling lakes – took his breath away. However, as he settled into his new consulting role, he couldn't help but notice that the corporate culture and values were eerily similar to those he had left behind in Dubai. The pursuit of profit still reigned supreme, and Zack still felt disconnected from his true passions.

During this time, Zack stumbled on a tight-knit surf town on Canada's coast. The relaxed atmosphere of the eco-conscious community captivated him. Here, he found himself surrounded by kindred spirits who shared his concerns about the environment and the urgency of adopting sustainable practices. It was in this inspiring setting that Zack decided to make a bold move.

He bade farewell to the corporate world, resigned from his high-paying job and embarked on a journey of self-discovery and reinvention. He embraced a simpler, more sustainable lifestyle in the small surf town. As he explored his newfound love for sustainability, Zack began to see that he could make a meaningful impact by combining his consulting expertise with his passion for preserving the environment. This fusion created a unique niche for him in the field of sustainability consulting.

Zack's journey was far from easy. It involved personal and financial sacrifices, and he faced uncertainty at every turn. However, his determination to align his career with his values and commitment to positively impacting the world kept him going. His story serves as an inspiring example for others who find themselves caught in the job-market dilemma – revealing that true fulfilment doesn't come solely from financial success but from pursuing a career that resonates with your heart and soul.

We hope that Yme's and Zack's stories provide you with some belief that you too can navigate the treacherous waters of the job market. Both narratives illustrate the power of aligning personal values with career vocation, proving that the job-market dilemma is not an obstacle but an opportunity to embark on a journey of self-discovery, chase your passions and become the author of your own transformative story. Yme, Zack and countless other career changers exemplify our incredible human capacity to redefine our paths and contribute meaningfully to the world.

Of course, not everyone faces such severe job-market dilemmas or requires such radical solutions. We have also met many young professionals who smoothly transitioned from one corporate to another within the same industry, and it turned out to be the right move for them. Some changed functions within the same company to match their ambitions; others found a better fit by moving to smaller or larger organisations in the same sector.

Your story is yet to be written. The job market represents a blank sheet on which to author a future that aligns with your desires. Whether it involves a bold move to a different country or simply a slightly different role within your current organisation, the choices are yours.

INTERNATIONAL VARIATIONS - THE IMPACT OF CULTURE

Now that we've explored the job-market dilemma, how it's intensified by the quarter-life crisis and the various forms it can take, let's delve a bit deeper into one final issue that significantly influences how you experience and cope with it: culture. The three authors of this book believe that the job-market dilemma exhibits nuanced variations across different regions and countries, shaped by cultural influences, educational systems and economic landscapes. However, although different countries exert different cultural pressures, the dilemma remains very similar: how can you forge your *own* path from the world of education to the world of work – and find the right match for you in the job market?

As Remon has moved around the world for his studies and work, he's encountered people who have experienced the job-market dilemma in very different ways, depending on the country they grew up in. He now works in Canada, amidst the gleaming skyscrapers of Toronto. It feels like a different planet, compared to the historic canals and picturesque old buildings of Utrecht, the small Dutch city that he left behind. When he first arrived, he was also struck by the very different mindset of his new friends and colleagues, compared to his classmates back in the Netherlands. North Americans seemed so much more focused on securing a high-paying job than on a healthy work-life balance compared to Europeans. Most of them had gone straight from their first degrees to graduate jobs too, rather than postponing their difficult career decisions by doing a master's. Remon speculated that this might be because of the more individualistic and capitalist culture of North America, which – so the story goes – places a strong emphasis on personal achievement and success. Or, he figured, it could simply be a side effect of the higher levels of student debt than in the Netherlands. Either way, he could see that the pressure to earn money – wherever it comes from – doesn't make it any easier to identify the right job for you. And it certainly doesn't make you any happier. It's just a different dimension of the job-market dilemma.

Even within Europe, there are strong cultural variations. Certain countries may prize specific fields of study based on historical traditions or contemporary economic needs. The national job market may reflect these preferences, with higher demand for certain professional skills above others. Additionally, some European educational systems encourage specialisation at an early stage, which may contribute to a more direct alignment between academic qualifications and career choices. As a Dutch national, for example, Remon felt it was only natural to pursue a master's before joining the world of work. But his partner Marina, who is from Spain, felt more pressure to find a stable job with long-term prospects. They both speculated that a riskier attitude to starting a career might be more prevalent in countries or regions that have a history of political or economic stability. Whatever the reason, the dilemma remains.

When Remon was studying at a Chinese university, he noticed that his Chinese classmates, most of whom were the only child in their families, seemed to be more focused on getting good grades and less on extra-curricular activities than the European students on his course. He concluded that China's one-child policy had probably created significant parental pressure to succeed and get a good job. In fact, the Chinese students reminded him of his friend Zack from Dubai (whom we met earlier in this chapter). Whether based on cultural or family tradition, the burden of expected success only complicates the dilemma further.

Remon wondered whether peer pressure might be the prevailing force in some cultures. In Canada, he met several Australian graduates, who were working their way around the world, temping or doing bar work as they went, before going back home to settle down to a career. From what they told him, this seems to be a tradition in their part of the world. No doubt they are gaining some great transferable skills and experience of different business environments, but postponing your job- market dilemma until an unspecified date in the future doesn't make it go away. Travelling for a few years might even close some career doors or make it harder to adapt to a more professional working culture.

By way of contrast, the young people whom Remon met in Benin, where he lived for a couple of months, seemed to be drawn to stay at home.

Graduating into the job market of a lower-middle-income economy with few prestigious universities left them with little opportunity to work abroad or to enrol on master's courses overseas. In fact, Remon knew some people who had abandoned studies they enjoyed just because a local job opportunity came up. Sometimes the decision is clear-cut, but the dilemma remains painful. Finally, in countries undergoing rapid economic growth there may be a bewildering surfeit of choice for young professionals!

Ultimately, it is impossible to generalise about the job market in different geographies, especially in today's fast-moving world. However, it is possible to generalise about the job-market dilemma: every culture has its own version! It follows that you should consider local factors, as you make your own decision. Understanding regional nuances is also essential for anyone embarking on an international career. If you can tailor your job market strategies to align with regional expectations and leverage cultural or economic factors, you will improve your chances of success and happiness, wherever you may be on Planet Earth.

THE PLOT THICKENS

Chapter 1 has laid the groundwork for exploring the intricacies of your own job-market dilemma. We've started by breaking down the essence of this phenomenon and explaining its link to the quarter-life crisis, a significant life phase marked by self-discovery and challenges. Our real-world examples show that the job-market dilemma isn't limited to specific industries but applies to diverse career paths. What's more, national or regional culture adds a further dimension to the dilemma. Nuanced variations across regions have a major impact on individual study and career choices.

Chapter 2 will deepen our exploration by examining the evolution of the job-market dilemma over recent decades and its variation across industries. Join us on this insightful journey through time as we uncover the historical perspectives and sector-specific dynamics that contribute to the ever-shifting landscape of today's career challenges.

CHAPTER 2
DISSECTING THE DILEMMA

When he graduated, Sikko made three serious applications before finally landing a job. His attempts spanned diverse sectors: an insurance company; a family-run conglomerate; and a retailer. The first two were brokered by personal connections, while the third was his own spontaneous endeavour. There was no deliberate strategy, just a combination of chance encounters and opportunistic decisions. It's a typical example of the – not uncommon – 'random' approach to the job market (see Exhibit 2.1).

A random job market strategy bypasses all the processes we describe in this book... First, analysing how you have developed as an individual during your studies and identifying your personal motivations for working. Second, exploring the world of work and the many sectors, roles and organisations it consists of, as well as looking ahead to future paths through the career landscape. And third, putting your conclusions together to choose where to send your first job applications. There are other strategies, of course, but they're all broadly similar: know yourself, know the job market – and find the best match you can. The random approach, on the other hand, consists of having no strategy: just applying for the first jobs that cross your path. This inevitably reduces your chances of getting the jobs you apply for. And worse, it also increases your chances of finding yourself in a thoroughly unsuitable job.

Exhibit 2.1: The random versus strategic approach to the job market

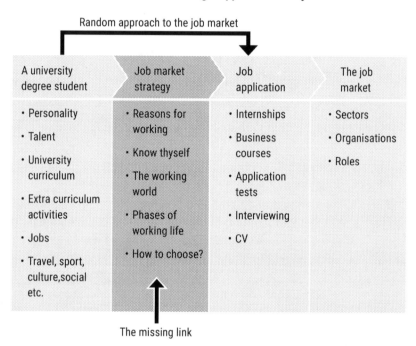

To be honest, the random strategy worked out quite well for Sikko. Not only was his first choice random, his second one was as well! After doing quite well in retail, he fell into executive search and fell for the people and the set-up of the firm he joined. He stayed for 30 years. And yes, you guessed right, Sikko is another of this book's co-authors. He's nearly three times as old as Remon (of Chapter 1) and he learned some important lessons during his long career in executive search. One of the lessons was that the job market has changed dramatically over time – with significant consequences for today's new entrants. This is precisely the lesson he would like to share with you in Chapter 2.

Think of it this way: Chapter 1 was all about *how* you're probably feeling, because of the job-market dilemma and the quarter-life crisis. Chapter 2 will give you more insight into *why* you're feeling this anguish so much more acutely than any other generation before you.

Even if you're not a fan of history or sociology, this chapter will help you when you're being bombarded with well-meaning advice from your elders, peers and social media... or worse, sinking under the weight of parental expectations. So, stick around with Sikko for a few pages more. You might just learn which advice to ignore, which to listen to and which to take with a pinch of salt. What's more, you'll gain some vital context for the rest of this book, particularly the sections that describe the job market and the patterns of working life. Best of all, this chapter will help you to avoid the random strategy that once served Sikko well... but can be risky in today's complex world.

First, we'll look at the differences between the generations alive today; next we'll look at the changes in markets, companies and organisations over recent decades; and then, we'll quickly cover the characteristics and evolution of a few key non-business sectors that also recruit a lot of graduates and young professionals.

DIFFERENT GENERATIONS HAVE DIFFERENT CHARACTERISTICS

Let's start by going back to the world of your grandparents or possibly great-grandparents. Born between the mid-1920s and early 1940s, the **Silent Generation** witnessed significant historical events like World War II and the subsequent growth of the welfare state. Members of this generation were shaped by the values of loyalty, hard work and conformity. This led them to follow traditional career paths, based on job stability and long-term commitment to a single employer. Brought up under conditions of frequent hardship and sacrifice of individual needs for the sake of collective good, the Silent Generation developed a strong sense of duty, discipline and resilience. Its members tended to embrace traditional roles and hierarchical structures in the workplace.

The children of the Silent Generation were the **Baby Boomers**, born between the mid-1940s and early-1960s. Members of this generation entered the workforce during a period of growing prosperity and societal change. Known for their strong work ethic and dedication, they usually pursued linear career trajectories. Under the influence of their parents, they were likely to stay with one company for an extended period, reflecting an era when loyalty, prized by their Silent-Generation managers, was reciprocated with job security.

Next came **Generation X**, born from the early-1960s to early-1980s. Members of this generation entered the job market around the dawn of the computer age and thus faced greater technological complexity in the workplace than their predecessors. By now, many societies were beginning to foster autonomy and individual choice, which introduced the concept of career flexibility. Competence was prioritised over seniority and paved the way for a more entrepreneurial mindset. While the Baby Boomers cherished stability more than career advancement, Generation X was increasingly motivated by financial gains and high performance.

Generation X was succeeded by **Generation Y** (also called the **Millennials**), born between the early 1980s and mid-1990s. By the time its members entered the job market, the digital age was in full swing, and it became ever-more normal to look abroad for career opportunities. At the same time, this generation was characterised by a desire for meaningful work, a preference for collaboration and a strong affinity with technology. Millennials often seek career paths aligned with their values and are more inclined to job-hop in pursuit of personal and professional growth, often at the expense of financial gain. Some people call them the 'Zap' generation because they behave in the job market as they did in front of the TV as children: if they don't like it, or it takes too long, they zap to the next thing. Some of them may even be zapping their way through this book.

Generation Z, born from the mid-1990s to the early 2010s, were the first true digital natives. Growing up in a hyper-connected world, they have strong digital skills and a global perspective. Members of this generation tend to prioritise diversity, inclusion and purpose-driven work, valuing jobs that allow them to make a positive impact on the world. So-called 'extrinsic' motivations (like money, job titles and status) recede into the background in favour of intrinsic, value-oriented motivations (like socially and environmentally responsible work). Individual truth-seeking seems to be the motive for many of their different characteristics: they don't define themselves by preconceived identities (they want to express their individual truths); they look for dialogue and different perspectives (they want to understand and integrate different truths); and they break with conventional wisdom (in search of something better).

Finally, there is already a **Generation A**, born between 2010 and today. Their parents are mostly Millennials, so no doubt they will be well educated, environmentally aware, socially conscious and even more tech-savvy than their predecessors. But it's still a bit early to predict their attitudes to work.

Of course, these classifications are sweeping generalisations that don't necessarily apply to all individuals. There is also debate over the cut-off dates and inevitably a great deal of blurring around the generational boundaries. However, there's no doubt that we are all collectively influenced by the social and technological progress that we experience, as well as world events, such as war, peace, and globalisation. What's more, over the course of the decades, there are pronounced trends in characteristics and preferences that span multiple generations. Among them, there is a clear progression from more extrinsic to more intrinsic motivations, from stability-orientation to flexibility-orientation and from strictly hierarchical organisations to more inclusive and egalitarian management structures.

From a more personal point of view, there is also a shift between the older generations, who were raised in an environment where they had to make either-or choices ('if you do this, you can't do that'), and the younger generations, who have grown up in a 'both-this-and-that' society. During your studies, you may well have thought you could have it all after graduation: a good income, a buzzing social life, challenging work, a sense of purpose, lifelong learning, social impact, organisational impact, family life, to name just a few. However, once you start working, you will increasingly come to realise that you have to make trade-offs. This book will help you decide why and how to make these tricky choices.

Even if you already know you only want 'some of it', don't underestimate the way the job market will shape *your* generation's career choices and, conversely, how generational change has shaped the job market and its organisations over the years – from the post-war period to the dawn of the 21st century and beyond. In order to understand where the shift in preferences over generations came from, let's run through recent decades once again, but this time with a focus on the changes in the working world.

THE SIXTIES AND SEVENTIES

Although the world was still recovering from war in the early sixties, society was rapidly rebuilding. Earning a living, job security and supporting the welfare state were important drivers in many countries. Life was relatively simple in those days, with a limited number of places on a limited range of university courses, and the labour market was relatively straightforward, with lifetime employment considered the norm.

Business consisted of larger multinational and national companies (the corporates of today) and more local SMEs (small- to medium-sized companies, often family owned and run). Large professional services firms (specialising in areas such as audit, strategy, law and executive search) were gaining importance alongside the public sector: civil service, education, healthcare and others. Ownership of all these organisations was pretty straightforward: they were either listed on the stock exchange, partnerships, family-owned or government-owned. In most countries, the utility and transport sectors (energy, water, airports, ports, railways, etc.) were in full public ownership.

Most companies operated outside the media glare. Shareholders and stakeholders did not voice opinions as strongly as they do today.

Executives were mostly unknown to the public, even sometimes to company employees. And non-executive directors, if they existed, were far less engaged compared to today.

Although few people could name the CEOs of the biggest corporations, like Shell or Unilever, these multinationals were growing in size and importance. In general, this expansion was achieved largely on the back of 'home-grown' talent — people who developed their entire careers within the same company from a young age. External recruitment of experienced people was rare.

From an individual point of view, the entire labour market was visible and revolved around employers within your home country. Applying to a foreign company was very rare. If you wanted an international career, an expat role through a multinational based in your home country was almost the only option.
Home or away, the organisation took care of you. A decent income was standard across the board, and career progression consisted mainly of internal promotion through fixed salary bands and levels of seniority. Executive search firms started to emerge in the sixties but initially played a modest role because of the limited number of external career moves available.

From the aspiring young professional's point of view, communication, and exchange of information with recent graduates, colleagues and parents was also very limited. You didn't share much with your peers or seniors, let alone commercially sensitive information or taboo details about your salary, which meant there was less social pressure than today. If you didn't know what anyone else was doing or earning, there was no incentive to compete!

Why was there so little exchange of information? Well, there are two obvious reasons. Firstly, the parents of these young professionals had experienced war, then helped to rebuild their countries and thus valued stability and predictability in their job choices. There wasn't a great deal to say about their work! Secondly, it was a lot more difficult than it is today to talk to people. Take Sikko, who was a student in Rotterdam during the 1970s. His parents lived 300 kilometres away in Groningen. Communication between them was infrequent, typically an occasional letter or a brief phone call every two or three weeks, each lasting only five to ten minutes due to the limited availability of coins for the payphone. This scarcity of contact meant that even if his parents had wanted to exert more influence or guidance over Sikko's academic journey – particularly when he failed his second year – their capacity to do so was minimal. In those days, parents were remote figures. Even if you studied at a local university, rather than leaving home, you were likely to keep different hours from your mum and dad and eat in the college canteen rather than the family dining room. Studying was the first step towards independence.

The first signs of a changing world became apparent around the dawn of the eighties, when the employment market became more complex and more opaque, and economic conditions were such that competition for simply finding a job became intense.

THE EIGHTIES AND NINETIES

The expansion of the global economy in the eighties created a new appetite for riskier investments. While the Dow Jones stock index hardly returned any inflation-adjusted profit between 1960 and 1980, it skyrocketed by over 1,000% over the next two decades. Fuelled by the rise of technology and services, a newfound sense of optimism and opportunity led key players in industry and politics to adopt a less conservative approach (finally culminating in the dotcom bubble at the turn of the millennium).

During the 1980s, much of the developed world, spearheaded by President Ronald Reagan in the US and Prime Minister Margaret Thatcher in the UK, reduced levels of both regulation and taxation, especially on capital gains. This in turn contributed to the birth of a new kind of financial industry, which turned the corporate world on its head with leveraged (euphemism for 'debt-powered'), high-risk-high-reward ventures. Businesses of all sizes were now evaluated based on their potential to yield short-term profits through restructuring, rather than long-term returns. While the 1980s saw the first billions pouring into private equity, this sum would rise to about US$100 billion at the dawn of the 90s and to a staggering US$4.1 trillion by 2024. The agenda was set: privatisation, deregulation and flexibilisation were the new norm.

The eighties foreshadowed developments that have since entrenched themselves in the mainstream: 'core business strategy' and 'shareholder value' became the drivers for managing corporations and smaller companies. New business concepts emerged, in tandem with the growing importance of venture capital and private equity, whereby the philosophy of 'going concern' was in many instances, replaced by 'value creation' within a 5–7-year span. The new 'owners' were less interested in developing people than in financial performance, but they were quite willing to splurge on rewarding employees for success through mechanisms like profit-related bonuses or share options.

Many companies decided to divest non-core businesses and acquire core business, which impacted organisational culture and led to an increased focus on the 'bottom line' and share price. As a result, employees came to be viewed as assets, hence the term 'human resources', which replaced 'personnel'. A side effect of this focus on performance was that star business leaders became public figures, supported by growing media coverage. Making money became synonymous with being successful.

Meanwhile, at the other end of the career ladder, young professionals faced new challenges. Instead of being offered a safe platform to develop workplace skills, graduate recruits were confronted with performance reviews, 'up or out' promotion pressure, bonus culture and job insecurity.

How did these young people respond? Well, if you no longer rely on your employer to guide your career, you have only one option left: manage your career yourself. And how do you do that? By comparing internal with external options. That's when networking and executive search came to the fore. Just as the new divestment and M&A strategies encouraged company leaders to call on executive search firms for help in finding and evaluating senior talent, so young professionals started building bottom-up networks through friends, colleagues, mentors, industry organisations and early relationships with executive search consultants. In short, there was a trend towards finding a sounding board for your career and gateways to external opportunities, even when you were still at entry level.

There were inevitably downsides to this development . The marketability of your CV became more important, so there was pressure to specialise early and play only to your strengths. Suppose, for example, your ambitions lay in sales and marketing. Whereas a sidestep into finance or HR might have made you a more balanced commercial executive, this was no longer seen as a viable option. Instead, it was perceived as 'weakening your CV' or 'a missed opportunity' – you could have added more sales experience instead. Recruiters and search firms were more than happy to play their part in this commoditisation of careers. Furthermore, the globalisation of the economy led to more international competition for jobs.

Parallel to these 'market developments', there were also changes in higher-education systems across the world: stronger emphasis on good grades on the one hand and a bewildering array of subject choices on the other. In some countries, this was linked to an expansion in higher education. In others, the driving force was greater specialisation at secondary school, which eliminated certain choices at university. In addition, increased pressure on universities for their students to complete degrees on time resulted in earlier entrance to the labour market and less opportunity for extracurricular activities – from sports clubs and music groups to memberships fraternities, internships and part-time jobs. Alas, for the young people concerned, the push for higher grades, early specialisation and shorter studies, did not allow much space for maturing as an individual, during those crucial years between the ages of 18 and 25.

The paragraphs above clearly represent an oversimplified explanation of two very turbulent decades and many, vastly different, individual experiences. Remember, the workforce in the eighties and nineties consisted of three generations: the tail end of the Silent Generation, the Baby Boomers *and* Generation X. In other words, society didn't have a *single* new way of operating. One thing was sure, though: while the previous decades were relatively simple times and their job markets relatively easy to navigate, by the early nineties that all had changed... foreshadowing the even bigger developments of the 21st century.

THE 21ST CENTURY

Of course, the fall of the Berlin Wall in 1989 and the introduction of the euro in 1999 were truly important events, but it's fair to say that, since the start of this century, the world has faced huge economic, financial, technical, political and social challenges. To name just a few: the dotcom bust that began in 2000, the 9/11 terrorist attack of 2001, the succession of conflicts in the Middle East, the 2007–2008 financial crisis, #MeToo, Black Lives Matter, the Covid-19 pandemic, Russia's invasion of Ukraine and all the while, growing concern about climate change, migration and – last but not least – the digitalisation of society. All these geopolitical, environmental, technological and economic threats have had major consequences for the job market, which represent opportunities and risks for both organisations and individuals.

But this is not all. From a job-market point of view, the new millennium brought even greater internationalisation of higher education and recruitment, as well as an even louder call for diversity, especially in terms of inclusion of women and minority groups. Equal opportunities are currently high on the agenda, and traditional gender roles and career patterns are being questioned more than ever before (although in some countries these ideas have been around for decades). Couples with so-called 'dual careers' are the norm, creating challenges for the individuals and organisations concerned, especially if at least one of the two careers takes an international turn.

All of the events and developments mentioned above have had an impact on how we live and work today. But with respect to work (and probably our private lives too), the rise of the digital society has been the biggest game changer. It affects every aspect of our existence. And now we have artificial intelligence (AI) to contend with, including ChatGPT and its competitors, which promises to change the pace, quality and efficiency of work even more radically.

First of all, take our methods and pace of communication. Starting with email and moving up the social media ladder, there is an overflow of information, to which the world wants us to respond instantly. With hardly any time to reflect, we have to react. For instance, in the past, law firms received letters by post and later by fax, so no one expected a response from their lawyer for at least a few days. Nowadays, an expert opinion is required immediately.

The digitalisation of business and society has not only put new organisations – such as Google, Apple and Meta – at its heart, but also changed business models – consider Amazon, PayPal, Netflix, Spotify, and many other examples. In fact, *all* organisations have had to adjust their ways of working, on the one hand to operate more efficiently and on the other hand to cope with new hitherto unimagined forms of competition. Traditional industries, such as financial services and retail, have suddenly had to cope with competitors born of technological possibilities – whether online shopping or fintech. Amazon changed the face of retail, while payment services, traditionally supplied by banks, are now hosted by the Adyens of this world.

Digitalisation also enabled remote working, which Covid then accelerated. This phenomenon will not go away and is beneficial for many employees and employers. The ultimate example is the digital nomad, who personifies the flexibility of modern work by operating from any location in the world, whether from the comfort of their home or a holiday resort – often with their exact whereabouts unknown to colleagues or clients. Again, there are upsides and downsides for young professionals. WFH (working from home) gives couples more flexibility for dual careers (both partners pursing their ambitions) but makes it harder for us all to stay connected to the organisations we work for and the people we work with.

Never before has the job market changed as drastically as it has since the beginning of this century. In the early 2000s, new multinationals emerged, seemingly overnight, whilst more traditional corporates had to adjust their portfolios, business models and working practices. Added to the pressure from digitalisation and shareholders, was the pressure from the media and public opinion to do good for society and the planet. Suddenly, traditional oil companies and their like fell out of favour among graduate jobseekers (and some investors). So did pharmaceutical companies... at least until Covid.

The digital possibilities of new business models and product–market combinations also created a whole new world of smaller entrepreneurial outfits. Not only have the numbers and types of organisations increased enormously; the way business activities get financed has also changed. Today, every option is available, from the more traditional public listing and family ownership to venture capital and private equity to informal investment and crowd funding. Almost every organisation today, in whatever form, has been transformed – if not created – by the digital revolution.

From the young professional's point of view, whether Gen Y or Z, the job market has far more choices to offer – in terms of sectors, types of organisations, size of company and geography – than when Sikko graduated all those years ago. And the same goes for the Baby Boomers and Gen Xs who have remained active in the world of work. For Gen Y and Z and soon Gen A, there are more and more study options available. Even traditionally vocational degrees – like law, medicine or engineering – are no longer seen as definitive choices. All this is, generally speaking, good news. However, there is a caveat. Too many options can leave people confused and insecure, especially when they lack clear guidance. In these circumstances, the random career strategy (which we warned against at the beginning of the chapter) becomes simultaneously more tempting and more risky.

There are several reasons why making the necessary choices has become particularly challenging. First, we live in an era of instant gratification. This expectation of instant fulfilment extends to study and career choices, complicating the decision-making process and creating a bias towards options that promise swift rewards. Second, we live in an era of hyper-communication. Trying to listen to the voices of parents, friends and society can be disorienting and pushes young people to make choices based on prevailing norms and expectations, rather than individual need.

The influence of parents is particularly complex, as we have observed through discussions with students during our classes. Parents mean well. They often encourage their children to pursue their passions and support their choices with words like, 'It's your life; we support every decision.' However, it's not just what parents say but their actions that truly set expectations. Despite mothers' and fathers' best intentions, children are acutely aware of their parents' unspoken desires.

Adding to this phenomenon is an extra layer of twenty-first century complexity. Parents today often view their relationship with their children as one of equals, almost like best friends. This perception is illusory. Children are hardwired to regard their parents as figures of authority and look for their approval, not just friendly advice. This discrepancy between perceptions also extends to how each group perceives the other's age. Parents see their children as slightly younger versions of themselves, minimising the perceived age gap. Conversely, children view their parents through a lens that accentuates the difference, seeing them as much older than they can ever imagine becoming!

Another huge element of uncertainty is the influence of social media. In this respect, the pressure of living up to others' expectations outweighs the possibilities of proper exchange about job market opportunities. For instance, LinkedIn and other social media encourage Generations Y and Z to compare themselves with their peers constantly. It's all too easy to find yourself saying: 'I was happy applying to a local bank, but everyone else is applying to Goldman Sachs.' The generational tendency to 'want it all' at the same time, leads many young graduates to 'zap' between several jobs within a few years of leaving university (as mentioned in Chapter 1).

Another new phenomenon is that young professionals are increasingly attracted to non-traditional environments, such as start-ups or even their own entrepreneurial ventures. Entrepreneurship is often considered cool, compared to working for a mainstream company, but this attitude can be based on gut feel, peer pressure and desire for autonomy, rather than on rigorous research and self-analysis.

So far, we've covered the dilemmas of today's job market through the lens of business. But the world is not only about business. Is it just as hard to make choices about working in other sectors, such as government, healthcare, education, the arts, sport and non-profit organisations? Or have these remained stable across the past few decades?

LOOKING BEYOND BUSINESS

Our original objective was to give you a historical overview of the non-business job market, similar to our description of business above. We started with three of the biggest non-profit sectors: government, healthcare and education. But we soon discovered that the variations from one country to the next made it very difficult to generalise in international terms. What's more, these three examples are just a drop in the ocean. Culture, sport, NGOs, local charities, trades unions, professional and industry bodies, utilities, employment services, law enforcement, research institutes, think tanks... the list goes on with increasingly diverse cases. Even within one country, it's almost impossible to make general statements about developments over recent decades that are true.

We'll return to the specific characteristics of these sectors in Chapter 5, when we look again at the world of work. But for now, we'll simply ask: have the non-business sectors been affected in the same way as the for-profit world by historical forces? And the answer is: yes and no.

From an organisational point of view, with a few exceptions, the not-for-profit sectors have been shaped by the key business megatrends, namely, digitalisation and the rise of the performance culture. Here's an example of the latter from the university world. After doing a PhD, most people do postdoctoral research or enter a tenure track, where they have to prove themselves in research and teaching for a period of several years. After that, there is often an 'up-or-out' situation, depending on the university and the conventions of the academic field.

However, while in business the megatrends of digitalisation and performance culture have led to new product concepts, industries and types of companies, the activities of the non-business sectors have – broadly speaking – continued to be organised in the same way they always were – especially in our three key examples of government, healthcare and education. The more traditional career patterns, based on gaining step-by-step experience and seniority, still prevail.

Let's take the specific case of becoming a clinically specialised doctor in Sikko's home country of the Netherlands. After your master's in medicine, you apply for an internship. If you can't get one, you may settle for a fellowship (same work, but not the same career path to becoming a specialist) and finally you have to find a permanent place as a clinical specialist. Apart from competing with others to get a place at that level, there's also a question of geography. You may have to move to a different region or city, which might be bad news for your partner's career... or your relationship. All in all, it takes an 'investment' of some 15 years to become a clinical specialist today – just as it always did.

Of course, there are arguments in favour of the kind of long-term career planning available in organisations like the civil service. It's nice to know that you're guaranteed to gain a lot of experience and that, once you've proved yourself at a certain level, you'll have a good chance of progressing to the next grade. The pension might be generous too! But from the perspective of a young person from Gen Y and Z, does this satisfy your need for flexibility, fast pace and instant rewards? As we'll see in the next chapter, it's tempting to embark on a public-sector career if you have a passion for serving society, but you also have to consider your own job and life satisfaction. It might be a better idea to apply to a charity, a social enterprise or even a commercial organisation with a strong mission statement to do good.

The same doubts hang over those who follow their passion into, say, sport – except that professional athletes have the opposite problem! Even if you get the gold medal you always dreamed of, your career will be short. You'll be forced to change jobs, whether you like it or not. And then, how will you use your sport toolbox to compete on the 'first job' playing field against applicants who are six to ten years younger than you? Admittedly, the option of turning professional is a comparatively recent option in most sports, but that doesn't necessarily make it a fulfilling future for Gens Y and Z. The rewards are potentially huge, but so are the risks – including the loss of other opportunities. Once again, it's important to know the long-term consequences of your initial career choice.

Professional sport isn't the only new (or nearly new) career option open to today's younger generations. Paths that once seemed unorthodox, like joining an NGO are increasingly accepted and even prestigious. If Baby Boomer Sikko had joined an organisation like Greenpeace, his parents and teachers might have raised their eyebrows and made comments such as, 'Couldn't you get a proper job?' But if Gen Z Remon had made this choice, he might have heard, 'Oh, great that you're working towards a more sustainable future!' The change in societal attitudes is due to the megatrend of rising awareness of the climate crisis (and other problems facing the human race).

Of course, there have always been unorthodox career choices with high prestige, like becoming a professional artist, actor or singer, for example. But as for professional sport, the high risks have to be considered alongside the rewards and status. And as for *all* career choices, the long-term consequences have to be taken into account.

One of the most significant long-term consequences of all is earning potential. And here, there's a historical trend about which it is possible to generalise. Over the past few decades, the rise of the performance culture – and, more specifically, profit-related benefits – has led to widening income gap between business and non-business careers. This only becomes more marked with seniority. The consequences for Gens Y and particularly Z therefore remain to be seen but are not to be ignored.

We'll return to the question of long-term implications of early career choices in Chapter 7, but for now, we'll leave you with two historical conclusions that may resonate with your own situation. First, in today's rapidly shifting landscape of technology, values and organisations, many non-business career options that were previously unacceptable or even non-existent are now open to young professionals – with the blessing of their parents! Second, young professionals have themselves been subject to a generational shift, which makes some traditional non-business choices, with stable long-term career paths, less appealing than they used to be.

For readers in a hurry or in need of a recap, our sweeping historical journey in this chapter is summarised in Exhibit 2.2.

SEEING YOURSELF IN A HISTORICAL AND GENERATIONAL CONTEXT

What should we take away from all this history? The most obvious lesson is that the job-market dilemma faced by today's young professionals is far more challenging than anything experienced by their elders. The world we live in today is much more complex – in terms of technology, economics, geopolitics and climate change – than ever before. And the number of opportunities available in that world – in terms of roles, industries, organisations and locations – is also greater than for any previous generation. This is particularly true in the private sector, but the public and non-profit sectors have also been transformed by many of these recent developments and strongly influenced by new business practices.

At the same time, Generations Y and Z are far more demanding than their predecessors. They want a job that checks all the boxes at once,

Exhibit 2.2: A brief history of the job market

Period	Environmental Factors	Generations at Work	Individual Experience
1960–1980	• Post-war rebuilding mentality • Diversification of business activities, spreading the risk • Little shareholder influence	• Silent Generation • Baby Boomers	• Job security • Opaque job market • Lifetime employment • No large income differences between various sectors
1980–2000	• Focus on core business • No guarantee of lifetime employment • Primacy of shareholder value • New business concepts (private equity, venture capital) • Top executives as public figures	• Silent Generation • Baby Boomers • Generation X	• Performance culture • CV building • Bonus culture
2000–present	• Digital society • Big events and issues (economic, political, climate, migration) • Greater transparency and availability of information • Rise of social media	• Baby boomers • Generation X • Generation Y • Generation Z	• Many choices in a complex world • 'Want it all' at the same time • More frequent career changes • Social pressure • New kinds of organisations and ways of working

including purpose, family, social life, professional development, impact, passion and income. To complicate their situation further, today's graduates are under more pressure than past generations, whether from their parents or – through constant comparison with others on social media – from their peers.

Yet one thing has remained the same. Just like the college leavers of the 20th century, 21st century graduates do not know themselves well enough to match their strengths, potential and aspirations to the bewildering array of possibilities in the job market. No wonder a random approach seems the only option.

Fortunately, there is another way! Better still, it's more effective and efficient than jumping into a randomly selected job with your eyes shut... then doing the same again the following year if you don't like it. We advocate a step-by-step approach, starting with an obvious – but almost never asked question. Why do you want to work? This is the question we will help you to answer in the next chapter.

CHAPTER 3
WHY DO YOU WANT TO WORK?

t's strange how few people ask themselves the fundamental question: 'Why do I want to work?' And even fewer try to understand the motivations behind their answer. We believe it is essential to address these issues before going any further in resolving the job-market dilemma (presented and analysed in Chapters 1 and 2). To put it simply, if you cannot define what you are looking for, how will you recognise it when you see it out there in the job market?

The danger in *not* understanding what motivates you to work is that you will unconsciously follow *other people's* motivations rather than your own. In the worst-case scenario, you will wake up one morning in ten years' time and realise you have spent a significant proportion of your career responding to incentives that have been placed, all too tantalisingly, along a route that you never meant to take in the first place.

This chapter aims to provide you with a compass for your journey by enabling you to identify the priorities that *you* want to guide you in your search. First, it will offer a way to sort your possible motivations into seven simple categories. Second, it will take you through each of these categories, working from the most extrinsic (or external) to the most intrinsic (or personal).

Although we encourage you to focus on the more *intrinsic* motivators, as these are the most relevant for sustained job satisfaction, please don't underestimate the importance of the *extrinsic*. If you figure out, for instance, that a high salary is more important to you than being truly passionate about the mission of the company you are working for, don't lie to yourself! It's better to be true to this realisation than to constrain yourself in a straitjacket of the motivations you feel you *ought to* have. Remember too that, getting an accurate picture of your own priorities is an ongoing process. Your motivations can – and probably will – change over time. The main thing is that you should not fall prey to deceiving yourself about why you want to work at any point in your career.

THE HIERARCHY OF NEEDS AND MOTIVATIONS

You might already have come across the hierarchy of needs shown in Exhibit 3.1, based on the work of psychologist Abraham Maslow[7]. Although he himself never drew such a pyramid, it's inspired by his ideas about the importance of self-actualisation and -transcendence. As he investigated the biographies of people who enjoyed extraordinary personal and professional success, he discovered a common pattern: all of them were constantly pushing to transform themselves and the world around them for the better. However, before they could reach this heightened state of growth, they first had to fulfil a succession of more basic needs that were all about seeking to reconcile deficiencies.

Over his long career, Sikko, has developed his own hierarchy of the seven main reasons why people want to work. He started work on this during his decades in executive search, informed by his experience and reading, and perfected it with the help of his students at the University of Amsterdam. Sikko's hierarchy of motivations for working appears in Exhibit 3.1, roughly mapped onto the equivalent levels in Maslow's hierarchy of needs.

In both hierarchies, the higher the level, the more intrinsic and less extrinsic the need or the motivation becomes. By the time we reach the top, our horizon has widened to become not only intrinsically meaningful but selfless.

Of course, it would be a misconception to think that human beings progress step by step through Maslow's needs (or indeed Sikko's motivations for working), opening up the next need only when the lower ones are all completely satisfied. Instead, our focus moves up and down the hierarchy all the time, based on our situation, and we are constantly operating on multiple levels at the same time. So, it's probably more helpful to think about the pyramid in terms of a gradient of average states rather than a series of steps.

Exhibit 3.1: Maslow's hierarchy of needs and your motivation for working

Maslow's hierarchy of needs		Why do you want to work?
Transcendence helping others to self-actualisme	Growth Needs	
Self-actualisation personal growth, self-fulfilment		Contribution to society
Aesthetic needs beauty, balancem, form, etc.		Impact
Cognitive needs knowledge, meaning, self-awareness		Personal and professional development
Esteem needs achievement, status, responsibility, reputation	Deficiency	Passion
Belongingness and Love needs family, affection, relationships, work group, etc.		Recognition
Safety needs protection, security, order, law, limits, stability, etc.		Sense of belonging
Biological and Physiological needs basic life needs – air, food, drink, shelter, warmth, sex, sleep, etc.		Income

Now let's look at each of the motivations for working in more detail (from the bottom up), with a view to identifying and prioritising your own answers to the question: 'Why do you want to work?'

INCOME

It's probably fair to say that, if money did not play a part, most people would make different life and career choices. All the same, it's an interesting thought experiment to contemplate what ignoring money altogether would mean for your decisions about your future.

Another interesting question is what 'income' means to you. Yes, it's earning a living, but what kind of living? Is it better, equal or less, compared to the financial circumstances in which you've been raised? Is it enough to fulfil your day-to-day needs? If so, what is the level of needs you aspire to? And will your expectations be different at the beginning of your career and later in life?

It goes without saying that there are income differences between sectors. Generally speaking, financial services, consultancy and multinationals pay higher salaries and bonuses compared to not-for-profit organisations or small-to-medium-sized companies. The differences are probably less marked at entry level but can become significant later on.

As we saw in Chapter 2, there are historical reasons for this. From around the 1990s onwards, employee stock-option schemes became a common source of income in addition to salary and bonuses. Thanks to funding from venture capital and private equity, start-ups as well as established companies began to introduce such schemes. For obvious reasons, this didn't happen in non-business organisations, although the public sector generally continued to offer generous pension schemes. In fact, until the 1980s, most employers, in both the public and private sectors, tended to focus on secondary benefits like pension schemes or health insurance and very little on variable pay, except for perhaps sales commission. In those days too, entrepreneurs tended to be people who wanted to 'work for themselves', rather than achieve stratospheric levels of wealth or retire at forty. These traditional entrepreneurs still exist, but a new breed has also emerged: founders who start their company to maximise the financial gains, usually by selling part or all of it, whether to co-investors, another company or, through an initial public offering, to anyone who wants to buy shares.

It's important to recognise that income is not something we think about only in absolute terms. One form of relative evaluation is to consider whether your income is 'fair' in return for your contribution to your employer or your society. As a social worker, for instance, you might generate a lot of value for the people you are serving, but you might become resentful about working in a chronically underpaid profession.

Of course, if we are honest with ourselves, 'fairness' is all about how much income we generate relative to people in other jobs – and most of all relative to our peers. Since the income levels in many organisations have become more public and salaries started to diverge more drastically in the for-profit sector, this factor has only risen in importance.

Comparing yourself to others seems to be intrinsic to human nature. In a famous study[8] from 1998, some 200 Harvard graduates were given two options and asked which they preferred:

Option A: Your current yearly income is $50,000; others earn $25,000.
Option B: Your current yearly income is $100,000; others earn $200,000.

Over half of the respondents picked option A, despite being explicitly told that the purchasing power of a dollar was the same in both scenarios. Thus, they revealed an important bias in the way we evaluate income: the material goods that we can afford to buy with our salary are not the only factor in our decision to aim for a certain pay range. As human beings, we are highly sensitive to our social context. The status connected to the number on our pay cheque matters as much as what we can buy with it.

This finding is closely connected to the paradox identified by economist Richard Easterlin, which states that long-term growth rates of wealth and happiness are not significantly related both among and within countries. Although economic growth over the past decades has allowed for much higher levels of material wealth in most of the world, the overall level of happiness that people report in surveys has remained practically unchanged over the years. On an individual level, although a pay rise leads to a temporary increase in (job) satisfaction, after a while, it's taken for granted and the *relative* pay grade becomes more salient again. Similarly, what seems to be fair within your own country, is not necessarily fair on an international scale, which might make you feel dissatisfied and even prompt you to consider working abroad. It seems that the so-called 'Easterlin paradox' is partially explained by our hardwired disposition to 'keep up with the Joneses'.

In short, income motivation has two major components: its absolute level and how it compares relative to environmental factors (as summarised in Exhibit 3.2).

Exhibit 3.2: Absolute and relative income

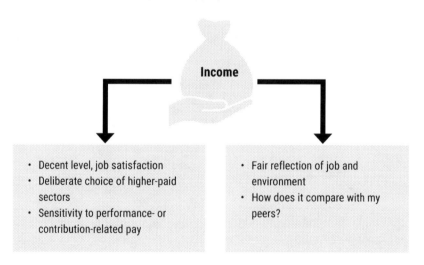

What can you personally take away from this? Our advice is not to jump to conclusions too early. Just take it in for now. Your feelings about income will become clearer once you have taken a closer look at the other reasons for working.

Before you do that, however, we'd just like to say one more thing about income. Of all the reasons for working, this is the only one that fulfils the basic needs to live on the bottom two levels of Maslow's pyramid. Apart from a very few exceptions, it's fair to say that every independent adult needs an income at some point in their lives — simply to survive in relative security. The bottom two levels of the pyramid are therefore uniquely associated with the decision to work or not, rather than any decision about the nature of the work you do. But who wants to work just to eat and feel safe? Let's move on up the pyramid...

SENSE OF BELONGING

When we asked our master's students at the University of Amsterdam Business School how important this driver was for them, it came out pretty low. In a way, that makes sense, if they interpreted it to mean 'feeling part of an organisation'. After all, many people are perfectly happy working on their own. They have freedom and flexibility, and still get to interact with clients, family and friends on their own terms. But is there more to the sense of belonging than simply feeling part of an organisation?

Granted, joining an organisation relates to the 'belonging and love' level of needs in Maslow's pyramid. To varying degrees, humans are social animals who enjoy doing things together.
In sport, for example, there are plenty of people who get more satisfaction from a team effort rather than an individual effort. On top of that, sports and group activities provide other opportunities for enjoyment: socialising and meeting new friends, for example.

If you take it one step further, achieving common goals is, for many people, an important reason to join an organisation. In smaller organisations especially, you can see your contribution very clearly, while in larger organisations, the common mission might have a bigger impact, even if you play only a tiny part in it (more about this later in the chapter).

All of the above reasons for being part of an organisation stem from the intrinsic wish to contribute to something together in an organised way. But there is still more to it. This intrinsic motivation can also help you to fulfil needs higher up the Maslow pyramid, such as personal growth. And most people benefit from working in an organised environment if they want to learn and develop. We'll talk much more about this in Chapter 7, but for now let's move on to the motivation we call 'recognition'.

RECOGNITION

Recognition relates very much to the peer, parental and environmental pressure, that we saw in Chapters 1 and 2. As mentioned there, it's not what your parents or friends say that counts; it's the implicit expectations revealed by their words and deeds that you need to understand.

Our classes at the University of Amsterdam Business School ranked recognition almost as low as 'sense of belonging', which was strange because they had chosen to do a highly regarded programme at an institution with an excellent reputation. What's more, they strongly identified with the job-market dilemma described and dissected in Chapters 1 and 2. We concluded that many of them didn't want to admit their need for recognition.

Generally speaking, the further away your choice is from your parents' or friends' frame of reference, the more likely you are to lack their recognition and feel their resistance. In the case of your parents, you may be getting mixed messages. They might well say, 'It's your choice.' But they will find other ways of expressing their true hopes or expectations. Some parents might secretly like you to follow in their footsteps, while others might want you to fulfil their own unmet ambitions. Either way, whether consciously or unconsciously, their feelings might well influence your choices.

When considering the relevance of others' opinions, it's important to make the distinction between parents, friends and superficial acquaintances. To start with the last of these, why bother about them? They're not interested in who you are and what you do, so don't take them too seriously. Friends, especially good friends, are different. They mean well and you may value their opinions. But are they able to have a *fair* opinion about what you should do and why? Like your parents, they're not always the best advisors. People who are close to each other emotionally are not always in a position to advise each other.

And it goes further than that. You may remember Yme, the booker and DJ from Chapter 1. Once he had found his way and told good friends of his parents what he was doing, he encountered two types of reactions. One was from people who were truly interested in what he did as a booker. The other was from people who meant well but made the killer comment: 'As long as you're happy...' – the implication being that Yme's work was inferior to a 'proper job'.

The example of Yme shows that it is not always easy to break away, partly because you don't know enough about the opportunities beyond your direct environment. But Yme's case also shows the importance of *recognising* the presence of environmental pressures. Only if you acknowledge your desire for recognition by friends, family and society can you avoid being guided by it.

If you're looking for insight into a specific sector or role, then by all means ask friends of your parents (or parents of your friends) with relevant experience. They will be able to provide you with valuable information. But beware of asking anyone (except a trained careers counsellor or a recruitment consultant) for *general* advice! By definition, someone with specific job expertise will give advice that is coloured by their own experience and quite often lacking an objective overview.

Sikko once spoke to a well-known CEO of a multinational, whose career had started in a small company, about the job-market dilemma faced by young people today. As a business leader, the CEO said, he was often asked for career advice by the children of his friends. And he always advised them to start at a small to medium-sized organisation. But just because it worked for him, that doesn't mean a small to medium-sized organisation is the perfect springboard for everyone. Smaller organisations have pluses and minuses, just like corporates, consultancies and NGOs. General advice worth trusting always takes a helicopter view, giving you an oversight of the various options.

During the first phase of your career, you will need to deal with well-meaning advice, peer pressure and other people's expectations. But will this go on for ever? Well, the environmental pressure to conform may diminish, but it's quite likely to be replaced by the quest for status, which may have a negative connotation, but is also expressed in more positive terms, such as 'ambition' or 'drive'. In some parts of the world, in certain sectors, you may even be considered insufficiently ambitious if you *don't* say that you're aiming to be CEO in your interview for a graduate traineeship.

For many successful people the quest for status is one of their main drivers. And indeed, ambition is an important asset, perhaps even a necessity to get the most out of yourself. There are people who need a 'North Star' to guide their career progression, without necessarily having a proper idea of what the top job involves. For a while, it's enough to be ambitious, but at some point, you'll need to understand a little more about yourself and the role you aspire to, otherwise you risk failure or unhappiness.

Remember, recognition is not just about hierarchical status. Sometimes, it's about joining a prestigious organisation, doing something worthwhile or having a desirable logo on your business card. If you're mad about football, you might be proud to join FC Barcelona in any role they'll recruit you for. If you're keen to serve the public cause, you might be proud of becoming a teacher or a civil servant. If you aspire to help save the planet, you might be proud to do an internship for Greenpeace. The value of the organisation or the activity somehow reflects on you. In the authors' opinion, if 'status' implies that you enjoy your role and you're proud of it, it's not a bad thing. It's only human to want recognition.

In the course of his work, Sikko once spoke to an executive, who felt that he was ready for a major CEO position. They discussed various, highly prominent options, before Sikko asked, 'Let's assume that you get one of these roles, but with one condition: no one will know that you're the CEO. Do you still want the job?' And the candidate reconsidered his motives. Were they the nature of the work, the challenges of the role, the power... or simply the public status?

In short, other reasons may be higher on your own personal list than recognition, and your quest for status may be unconscious, but don't underestimate the importance it will play in your early (and later) career decisions.

PASSION

When it comes to choosing a career, the most common advice is probably to 'follow your passion'. Again, this is usually well meant but difficult to put into practice, not least because so many options come into play (see Exhibit 3.3).

Is it a particular sector or an activity that you feel passionate about? Or is it the purpose, culture and people of an organisation? Or the intellectual challenge? And do you really need *passion* to get enthusiastic about something? It's difficult, verging on impossible, to find your passion in a working world you do not know very well.

As a consequence, many young graduates turn to a job or working environment they have witnessed in some way: teacher, police officer, airline pilot; a company that makes a product and service that they use; famous charities like Médecins Sans Frontières or the Red Cross; their parents' or older friends' professions. It's tempting to join or stay in a world you think you know. But the reality is not always how you expect it to be.

Take the example of two professional basketball players whom Sikko once advised. They loved their sport and were certain they wanted to stay in it after they retired from playing. Sikko tried another of his thought experiments with them: 'Let's assume that your team, the club, the level and the facilities stay the same. But the sport isn't basketball;

Exhibit 3.3: Follow your passion... but where?

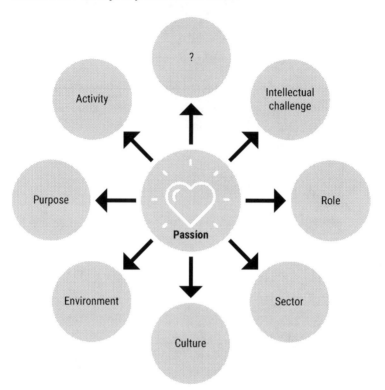

it's volleyball.' Their response was spontaneous: 'That sounds just as good.' In other words, your superficial convictions about where your passion will lead you are likely to be biased towards the familiar. And the truly important aspects of your dream job may not be obvious to you. Even when you think you know your passion, you still can be misled by irrelevant details into having tunnel vision. In the case of the two basketball players, their true passion turned out to be not basketball but professional team sports.

For most young professionals, however, the main issue is that they can't translate activities that they enjoy into a job, an organisation or a sector. Even if they're able to define what they most like doing, they will find it impossible to relate that to a working environment they do not know.

Here's another real-life example – but at the same time very different from Yme's story.

Bruce had just obtained his master's in psychology. During his studies, he had done quite a lot of DJing. He'd got to know the club scene and loved it, so it would have made sense to pursue a career as DJ or to find another role in the music business. However, he wasn't 100% sure, so he started to look at other options and came across an opportunity at Adyen, at that time an emerging player in payment transactions. Bruce didn't consider himself very commercially minded and didn't have much natural affinity with financial services. However, he was attracted to the entrepreneurial culture, the fact that the company was still at an early stage and the 'just do it' mentality. He joined and did very well, even though he had to take his career progression and management development into his own hands. To his great surprise, he enjoyed his new career immensely. If someone had told him during his studies that his first job would be in financial services, Bruce would never have believed it.

The example illustrates that when you have an open mind and are prepared to explore, you can come across an environment that has similarities with the sector you're naturally inclined to, but in a totally different field. In this case, a financial-services disruptor turned out to have the same non-traditional, non-hierarchical and entrepreneurial culture as the music business. It was the environment that counted for Bruce rather than the product or service.

The lesson is that it makes sense to 'unpeel' your passion and find your underlying motivation. For some people, it's the day-to-day activity that matters; for others it's the environment, the role or the purpose. There's no right or wrong – and no need to feel guilty if you don't have a passion at all. In any case, it will be easier to assess the question of passion, once you have read Chapters 5, 7 and 8, and have a clearer picture of the working world.

PERSONAL AND PROFESSIONAL DEVELOPMENT

Who does not want to grow and develop? For some people, learning is an end in itself, while for others, it's the means to achieve other goals, such as income, recognition and impact. Whatever the underlying reason, almost all young graduates say they are looking to develop both personally and professionally. But when you ask them for more detail, their answers become vague. 'I want to be good at something', 'I seek new knowledge and skills', 'I'd like to learn from others', 'My goal is to develop into a manager', 'I love to discover different cultures'... and more. This imprecision is related to their limited knowledge of what working is all about.

They're right about one thing, though: personal and professional development is especially relevant for the first phase of your career. The trick is to be aware of what, where, when and how you can satisfy your desire to develop. Let's start by making a simple distinction between *content*, such as knowledge or skills and *behaviour,* such as personal discipline or effectiveness (see Exhibit 3.4).

Exhibit 3.4: The two faces of personal and professional development

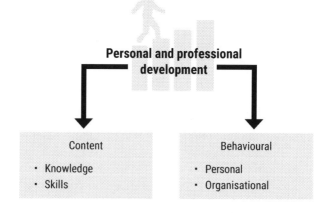

'Content' learning has two main varieties: knowledge and skills. Knowledge can take many forms. It can be about a subject, an organisation, an industry, a sector or a job, to name just a few. A skill goes beyond mere knowledge by also combining it with, talent, interest, intellect, instinct and practice and tends to create a more unique advantage than knowledge. The variation of skills is huge: a carpenter or a footballer's practical skills are very different from an IT expert or a strategy consultant's analytical skills.

Knowledge and skills particularly appeal to Generations Y and Z, who are known for seeking instant gratification. Today's young professionals measure whether they have learned enough on an almost daily basis. And content learning is easier to measure in the short term than behavioural learning. To fully understand how and when you have acquired behavioural effectiveness takes time. So don't be misled in your choices by seeking only learning that can be easily defined and measured.

We say this because behavioural learning is probably the most important element of your personal and professional development. No doubt you already know someone who is a technical expert but has problems interacting with other people and is therefore not as effective as they could be. In our experience, whenever senior appointments are made public, the justification is always that this is 'someone with the right expertise for the job'. But when someone doesn't work out it's almost always because of the way they behaved. As one of Sikko's colleagues in executive search liked to say, executives are hired on the basis of their CV and fired because of their behaviour.

Everyone agrees on the importance of behavioural development, but few people are explicit about what constitutes 'good behaviour'. Expressions like 'good listener', 'empathetic and engaged' and 'hits the right tone' are a start, but they don't fully capture what we're talking about. In a working environment, just being a nice person who's easy to relate to and get along with is not enough. What are the true differentiators?

The answer depends on your goals. Differentiators of behaviour are directly related to your ability and effectiveness in realising your goals. In the first phase of your working life, your behavioural development is likely to be more focused on *personal* effectiveness, but as you progress into your mid-thirties and beyond, organisational effectiveness will be the main factor in achieving your objectives.

During the many executive appointments Sikko has been involved in, he has identified several basic principles for personal effectiveness. Exhibit 3.5 presents the ten most important.

Exhibit 3.5: The ten commandments of personal effectiveness

- Be on time (for work, meetings, etc.)
- Get things done (deliver *what* you agreed to – and maybe more – *when* you agreed to – and maybe sooner)
- Understand where the bar is (i.e., the quality expected of your deliverables)
- Communicate if you are not able to deliver (it happens, but let others know in advance)
- Be prepared (research and thinking ahead are key)
- Be responsive (react to emails, calls and messages in a timely manner)
- Show appreciation (thank colleagues and clients for advice, hospitality, etc.)
- Understand what drives / motivates people on the other side of the table (before voicing your own view)
- Be prepared to go the extra mile (hard work and commitment)
- Show determination (overcoming setbacks is crucial to your development)

These ten commandments are something anyone can master, although they will come more naturally to some than others. They are not related to specific skills or knowledge, but it is critical that you learn to obey them in the first phase of your working life. If you don't develop your basic personal effectiveness early in your career, chances are you never will!

That said, personal effectiveness is not always a top priority for young professionals. In their defence, in today's world with its oversupply of information and communication, it's not always easy to follow these simple rules. And living by the ten commandments may be less important for a few exceptional people, such as talented artists or solo musicians, than it is for the rest of us. For most readers, however, developing personal effectiveness will be essential, because it's the basis on which you'll build your *organisational* effectiveness during the later stages of your career.

At this point, we won't say much more about organisational effectiveness, because it's less relevant to the early stage of your career. It's largely about achieving your goals *through* your interactions with other people, whether your direct reports, peers, bosses, customers or other stakeholders. In the next phase of your working life, you'll be confronted with complex situations beyond your control, but of a different magnitude and with a different level of responsibility, compared to earlier in your career. You'll have to integrate knowledge, skills and behaviour into a holistic response, whilst taking important decisions – sometimes multiple decisions simultaneously! And you won't have all the time and information you really need.

We'll revisit the concept of organisational effectiveness in subsequent chapters of this book too – just as we hope you'll do throughout your career.

IMPACT

Making an impact is high on the list of motivations for working among today's young professionals but, once again, it begs further questions: 'What exactly do you mean by impact?' 'Are you sure you're not just saying that because everyone else does?' 'Can you really expect to have an impact from day one?' Just as for personal and professional development, it helps to break 'impact' down into its component parts (see Exhibit 3.6)

Exhibit 3.6: The two faces of impact

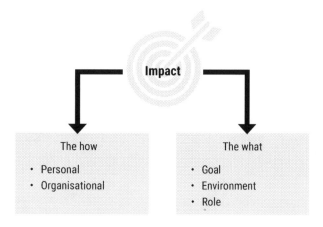

First, let's look at *how* impact is achieved. Is it direct and personal? Or indirect, maybe through an organisation? Greta Thunberg has made a powerful personal impact on public awareness of the climate crisis, while Greenpeace has made an organisational impact. Like Greta Thunberg, a carpenter, doctor, architect, musician or footballer, has a direct impact on individuals, such as customers, patients and clients, and/or groups, such as local residents, audiences or fan clubs. These are all examples of jobs where individual performance achieves some kind of end result.

It's the same for lawyers, who are usually asked for advice because of their specific expertise and reputation. The value they create impacts their clients directly. When Sikko worked in executive search, he too had specific expertise and – he likes to think – an excellent reputation. However, his impact was *indirect*. He didn't take the final hiring decision, but the candidates he and his colleagues found – whether business executives, museum directors or secretary generals – sometimes transformed the organisations he helped to recruit them to.

Generally speaking, at the beginning of your working life, your impact will be limited to your direct environment, for example colleagues and direct contacts outside your organisation. As you progress, your impact *within* the organisation will increase and so will your contribution to the external impact of the organisation as a whole.

The second distinction with regard to impact relates to *what* you wish to achieve. Is it to raise awareness of a subject close to your heart, like the climate crisis? Is it to satisfy shareholders, by working in private equity or for a listed company? Is it to make people happy, as artists and athletes do? Is it to transform an industry, as Mark Zuckerberg and Elon Musk did? Is it to help people in need by working for an organisation like the Red Cross or UNICEF? In other words, the 'what' is not just about the goal, but the working environment and the role.

Whatever your desired impact, we recommend that you take the two angles of 'how' and 'what' into account. Just wanting to make a difference will not help you greatly in making your career choices. You need to be more specific. In the end, *all* jobs are about making an impact of some kind. That's why people are paid to do them.

So far, we have looked at impact as a goal in itself. Now let's move on to a more altruistic type of impact.

CONTRIBUTION TO SOCIETY

For many people, especially members of Generations Y and Z, making a meaningful contribution to society, in whatever form, is an important driver. But the question of *how* to contribute to society through your job is a dilemma in itself.

The dilemma can be resolved by taking two different but related approaches. The first is to distinguish between making a *deliberate* choice to contribute to society by joining an organisation that has a direct social impact (such as a government department, an NGO or a charity), rather than an organisation (like a profit-making company) that has only an indirect social impact. Working for the government housing department suggests a deliberate choice to contribute to society; joining a construction company does not. But if that construction company builds low-cost housing and helps to solve the national shortage of accommodation, then you are still serving society, even though you are also serving the company's shareholders. It's just that your choice wasn't necessarily driven by your social conscience. And your service to society might have been entirely accidental.

The second approach is to analyse the various ways in which contribution to society can manifest itself. Broadly speaking, there are four main categories, although there is some overlap between them (see Exhibit 3.7).

Exhibit 3.7: Four ways of contributing to society

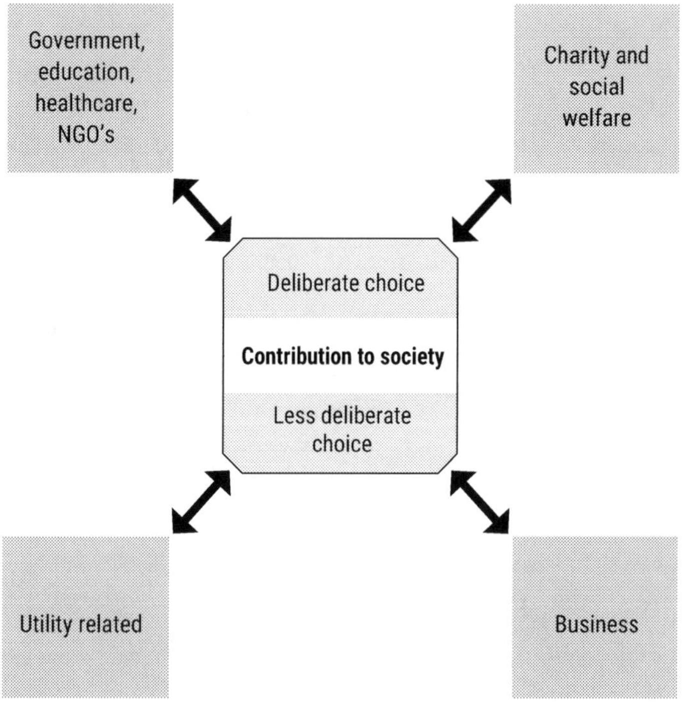

Government, education, healthcare, NGO's

Charity and social welfare

Deliberate choice

Contribution to society

Less deliberate choice

Utility related

Business

People who choose to work in government, education, healthcare or NGOs will almost certainly have a strong underlying motivation to serve the public cause. Of course, the nature of that motivation will not be identical for every person or even within every part of the public sector. To take just one area of government, the justice system creates a fairer and safer society. Good education, meanwhile, helps people to develop themselves. And good medical care leads to longer and happier lives and Greenpeace helps in protecting our climate. All of these sectors bring economic and other benefits to the world as a whole.

Charity and social welfare are more related to helping people with basic needs, both at a national and international level. The variety of organisations involved is wide, ranging from a local care home to a global aid agency. So, if your deliberate choice to contribute to society is motivated by human wellbeing, you have many options.

Utility-related sectors include transport, ports, energy, water and communication infrastructure – the mechanics that enable society to function. Although many of these activities have been privatised over the last 40 years, the government still retains significant control in most countries. And many young professionals consider the organisations involved as social-impact employers, even if they are technically 'businesses'.

Business more broadly is much more complicated to dissect and to analyse in terms of contribution to society. There are many sectors and roles that contribute indirectly to society but are often viewed as having a negative impact. Forty years ago, graduates flocked to join oil and gas companies because they literally fuelled the world economy; today, we still rely on them to drive our cars and heat our homes, but they are shunned as employers by some young people because of their carbon footprint.

If you are responsible for products or services that are in high demand, do you automatically contribute to society? Have Bill Gates and Jeff Bezos contributed to society by driving economic growth? Does a sports or cultural performer contribute to society? Do biotech start-ups with new healthcare innovations contribute to society? Is someone responsible for sustainability at Tata Steel, helping to save the planet and human society? Finally, what about the arms business? Does it destroy society by enabling war and destruction? Or does it protect the most important social asset of all: freedom?

The answers to such questions are not simply 'yes' or 'no'. They illustrate that there are many ways of contributing to society, which may or may not play a role in your own career choice. The main thing is that you don't dismiss sectors and companies as worthless to society, without considering the hidden contributions that they make. Even more importantly, reflect on what matters to *you*. How direct does your contribution to the greater good really need to be?

UNDERSTANDING YOUR OWN MOTIVES FOR WORKING

Before reading beyond this point, put the book down for a moment and reflect on which parts of this chapter stood out most to you. And which resonated least? Ask yourself: 'If I am completely honest with myself, which of these motivations for working applies to me? It's crucial that you realistically assess what *does* motivate you and not what *should* motivate you. Don't deny that recognition matters to you, just because you think it shouldn't. Analyse instead *how* it matters to you. And if earning more than your friends is important to you, don't tell yourself (and them) that you only want to 'make an impact' and 'contribute to society'.

If it's any consolation, we did some empirical research with our students at the University of Amsterdam Business School and discovered that the motivation of income came second only to opportunities for personal and professional development (see Exhibit 3.8).

Interestingly, income is located much lower in the augmented hierarchy of reasons to work shown in Figure 3.1 (see beginning of chapter) than personal development, yet both seem to be very important for most of the young people we surveyed. But overall, as we move down the ranking of our students' reasons for working, we seem to move from the higher levels of the pyramid to lower levels.

Exhibit 3.8: The seven reasons why our students wanted to work

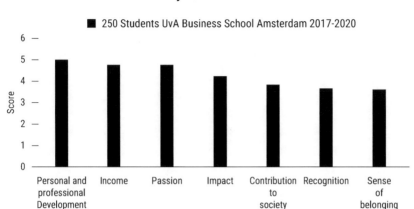

Our mini study is backed up by a 2022 survey by Deloitte[9] about reasons for working. Over half of Gen Z respondents suggested that they were motivated by opportunities for growth, compared to only 28% of Gen X and only 17% of Boomers. In fact, in these kinds of surveys, growth opportunities consistently rank in one of the top spots for recent graduates. Is this because, by developing yourself, you stand a better chance of getting a more senior position with higher pay? Or does it reflect a desire to learn for learning's sake, without having a clear idea where it may lead to? Sikko's personal feeling is that both reasons are valid for Generations Y and Z.

However, priorities can shift in times of uncertainty. Another survey conducted by the recruitment company RippleMatch[10] found that compensation and benefits became more important at the height of the pandemic compared to both pre- and post-Covid. This matches our observations about Maslow's hierarchy at the beginning of this chapter: deficiency needs can take precedence over growth needs in times of crisis. Similarly, you can expect your own motivations to evolve over time, as your priorities in life change.

BE HONEST WITH YOURSELF

The important lesson to take away from this chapter is that you must be truthful to yourself about the forces that motivate you at every point in your career, particularly when you are making a move in the job market. Don't be influenced by others – including your friends, parents and your former selves! Of course, it's easy to read surveys about other people's reasons for working, but it's tricky to read the inner workings of your own mind. That's why the next Chapter is all about getting to know yourself.

CHAPTER 4
KNOW THYSELF

By now, you are beginning to be an expert! Thanks to Chapters 1 and 2, you understand the job-market dilemma that you are facing and some of the reasons — both psychological and historical — *why* this dilemma is so hard to resolve. Thanks to Chapter 3, you know *how* important it is to take a methodical approach to finding your first 'proper job' and *what* kinds of reasons guide personal career choices. And in Chapter 4, you are going to develop your expertise in perhaps the hardest discipline of all: self-knowledge.

When the authors of this book first started designing their course on career choice at the University of Amsterdam, they knew that they would have to include some kind of psychological assessment tool — not just as a starting point but as a continuous guide throughout their students' professional journeys. After all, how can you begin to know whether a role, profession, organisation or industry is the right fit for you, unless you have taken a few basic measurements. You wouldn't buy a pair of jeans without knowing your size, so why would you jump into a job without knowing yourself?

The personality test we chose is called the AEM-Cube. It's a bit different from other psychological tools in that it isn't *just* about introspection.

The AEM-Cube is about aligning an individual's needs with those of their team or their environment. It evaluates how people navigate the complexities within their ecosystem and recognises that this ability develops over time and with experience. You can probably already see why it's so suited to resolving the job-market dilemma.

Another reason we chose the AEM-Cube is that it's been used globally by tens of thousands of individuals, teams and organisations to harness cognitive diversity for success in a vast variety of situations. Based on research by Dutch professor and psychiatrist, Peter Robertson[11], and developed by the consultancy firm that he founded, Human Insight, it's a proven assessment tool. It provides genuinely helpful insights about your strengths and how to leverage them for success in a role or organisation – and before that, in your applications and interviews.

Ron, one of the authors of this book, would also like to confess a further – personal – reason for choosing the AEM-Cube. Over his long career, he has always worked in business, but with a preference for international assignments and distinct projects, such as turnarounds, spin-offs and takeovers. Gradually, he gravitated away from corporate roles altogether and developed a portfolio career, covering consultancy, board memberships, research, teaching and writing. It was only when he discovered the AEM-Cube that he really understood *why* his career evolved in the way it did. As a highly 'exploratory' person, he had a fundamental need for change. He needed people, but was also 'matter-oriented', that is he needed to keep learning and gaining new knowledge. And, while he was good at building relationships, he also didn't mind a bit of conflict or eventually moving on to form new relationships. Most of all, he didn't mind juggling with complexities – managing different kinds of work within a hectic schedule.

But that's enough about Ron... let's get started on the AEM-Cube and what it reveals about *you*.

THE AEM-CUBE BASICS

The AEM-Cube is a distinctive assessment tool that zeroes in on the enduring personal qualities of an individual, such as key talents, values, interests and innate drivers. Its primary objective is to delve into the deeper, more persistent aspects of personality that significantly influence behaviour. Unlike tools focused on evaluating dynamic elements like skills or knowledge – whether factual knowledge acquired through formal education or experiential knowledge specific to an industry or market – the AEM-Cube operates on a different plane. It ignores transient competencies and doesn't dwell on cultural factors, such as geography, gender, age, ethnicity or lifestyle (even though these too are often things that don't change). The AEM-Cube's unique focus is on the intrinsic qualities *of an individual* that are *stable over time*. This approach enables a profound exploration of how your innate preferences influence your behaviour and decision-making processes in both your professional and personal life.

The AEM-Cube tackles three fundamental questions, each corresponding to an axis that enables you to map your innate preferences in a particular direction:
- Am I driven more by people or content? ('Attachment' axis)
- Do I flourish in stable or changing environments? ('Exploration' axis)
- Do I express myself or integrate my actions with others? ('Maturity in Complexity' axis).

Think of your AEM-Cube profile as a relative score, a dynamic comparison with others who have completed the assessment over time, rather than a fixed measurement on three absolute scales. By the end of the chapter, you will be able to see roughly which point in this three-dimensional space (see Exhibit 4.1) that you occupy.

Before diving into the depths of the AEM-Cube, it is also essential to distinguish between innate (instinctive) behaviour and learned behaviour. Your positions on the AEM-Cube's attachment and exploration axes are defined by innate behaviour and thus remain relatively constant

Exhibit 4.1: The three axes of the AEM-Cube

throughout your life. However, it is possible to develop your maturity in complexity and thus to move your position on this axis over time.

ATTACHMENT AND EXPLORATION: THE BASE OF THE CUBE (THE A AND E AXES)

Now let's look more closely at the two axes that together form the floor of the AEM-Cube: attachment and exploration.

On the one hand, the attachment instinct is primarily directed at preserving your safety and creating the conditions for exchanging knowledge. On the other hand, the exploration instinct nearly always combines fear of the unknown *and* hope for the future. Over millions of years, human progress has been defined by the way we cope with our fear of leaving the familiar in the hope of improving our lives. The instinct to explore is directed at anything that's new, previously unknown and available only *outside* your immediate environment.

A good understanding of these two instinctive behaviour patterns will help you not only to understand your own personal preferences but also the demands of any role in any organisation at any given point in time. If you play your cards right, you'll be able to align your personal preferences with the demands of a role – and thrive.

We're not saying that you *can't* thrive in a role that aligns with a *different* AEM-Cube position. In fact, you might be very effective and successful. You may even develop skills, knowledge or routines that overcompensate for your innate shortcomings in a specific role. These learned behaviours may be so convincing that your colleagues are totally unaware of the fact that they don't align with your inherent preferences.

The trouble is that prolonged misalignment can be problematic. In low-stress situations or when the discrepancy is minor, you might do well for quite a while. However, as stress levels rise, learned behaviours often give way to natural inclinations. You risk burning out from overstress or jeopardising your career through underperformance. That's why it's important to align your career choices as closely as possible with your intrinsic AEM-Cube profile for success and well-being in the long term.

Having said all that, it's also important to recognise that the basic instincts of attachment and exploration are interdependent, as the following example will make clear.

Picture this: you have a new colleague at work, fresh from university. She is just about to finish her first week on the job, and you have invited her to join you to the weekly Friday-evening drinks.

As 5 pm rolls around, the office buzzes with anticipation. You both pack up and head to the local bar, a familiar haunt for you but uncharted territory for her. The bar is lively, humming with the sound of conversation and music. You are in your element among so many familiar faces, while your colleague looks around, feeling out of place. Suddenly, a work friend pulls you aside to discuss an urgent matter and without meaning to, you turn away from your new colleague. She lingers close by, looking a bit lost and uncertain. She is hoping for a chance to join the conversation but can barely get the gist. As time passes, you become engrossed in your discussions, inadvertently turning your back on her as more colleagues join in.

Meanwhile, the new girl, still hovering nearby, starts to scan the room. She is looking for a familiar face, anyone she might have met during her first few days. Finally, she takes a bold step and decides to venture out into the crowd. That's when she hears her name called out. It's someone she met by the coffee machine earlier in the week. She is welcomed into a group of friendly faces, introduced to them all and soon, she is sharing stories and laughing along. Her initial unease melts away as she becomes part of the lively conversation. She occasionally glances over to you, sharing a smile or a wave, to let you know she is okay.

As the evening winds down, you approach her to say you are heading home. She is brimming with newfound confidence, smiling broadly and telling you about her plans to grab dinner with her new acquaintances.

This experience encapsulates the dynamics of attachment and exploration. Initially, your colleague clung to the safety of your presence in the unfamiliar setting. The overwhelming newness made her cautious, preferring the security of staying close to you. However, as she gradually acclimatised and her discomfort subsided, her exploratory instincts kicked in. She began to engage with her surroundings, slowly at first, then with growing confidence, immersing herself in the social fabric of the evening. Her periodic checks with you represent the attachment system at work, seeking reassurance while venturing into exploration. This simple yet telling example sheds light on how we navigate new environments, balancing the safety of attachment with the thrill of exploration.

ATTACHMENT EXPLAINED: PEOPLE VERSUS MATTER

The attachment system is a fundamental aspect of human interaction, evolving to forge stable bonds that historically ensured survival by sticking together and exchanging knowledge. In the office drinks scenario, the new colleague relied on you as a source of security in an unfamiliar setting. This reliance exemplifies a deep-rooted attachment response, a bond triggered by the need for safety in new environments.

In our early years, attachment typically centres around our parents, who serve as a refuge and symbol of safety. As we mature, our sphere of attachment expands. Our reliance on physical proximity diminishes, allowing for more abstract forms of connection. In the story about the Friday-night drinks, your new colleague wants to keep you — literally — in sight, just as a child does with its parents in a strange situation. But with age and experience, we no longer need our family and friends constantly near us. As long as we are aware of each other's existence, it's enough to stay in touch by Zoom or WhatsApp, whenever we need support or want to share news.

As we get older, we also develop a different kind of attachment – to 'matter', that is to ideas, objects or content. The AEM-Cube measures attachment along a spectrum from people-attachment to matter-attachment. People-attached individuals draw comfort and motivation from human interactions, whereas matter-attached individuals find security in content, concepts or objects.

Before we dive into the details of what that means, we encourage you to look at the table below. Here we have listed some characteristics of people at both ends of the spectrum. Do you recognise elements in yourself or close colleagues or friends?

People attached	Matter attached
Use content in their interaction with people. *Example: A team leader uses project results to encourage team bonding and celebrate collective achievements.*	Use people to make sense of / apply content. *Example: An engineer consults with various expert colleagues to refine a technical proposal.*
Act on feelings (of others). *Example: A manager adjusts the project timeline after noticing the team's stress and fatigue.*	Act on knowledge / facts (known by themselves). *Example: A financial analyst decides on an investment based on thorough data analysis.*
Are convinced through (the opinion of) people. *Example: A colleague might change their stance on a project approach after hearing the team's collective opinion.*	Are convinced through knowledge / facts. *Example: A colleague remains steadfast in their project plan, citing data and previous case studies as justification.*
Say: 'I think so'. *Example: A colleague suggests a new approach in a meeting based on their gut feeling about the team's dynamics.*	Say: 'I know so'. *Example: A software developer is certain about a coding solution due to their extensive experience in the language.*

Might be right when they claim something.	Will be right when they claim something.
Example: A colleague predicts the success of a marketing campaign based on their intuition about customer preferences.	*Example: A colleague accurately forecasts budget requirements based on their detailed analysis of past financial data.*

When exploring, people use an emotional beacon of safety. If you're highly people attached, people will be your 'go to' beacon; if you're highly matter attached, your 'go-to' beacon will be things, techniques, ideas, etc. The extent to which you are matter or people attached is shown in the attachment axis that runs from the front to the back of the AEM-Cube base (see Exhibit 4.2). You can be at one of the extreme ends or right in the middle of the axis, in which case you will see both matter and people as equally important beacons of safety. But most people are positioned somewhere between one of the extremes and the mid-point on the scale, some leaning more towards people attachment, while others are more inclined towards matter attachment.

Exhibit 4.2: The matter-attachment–people-attachment axis of the AEM-Cube

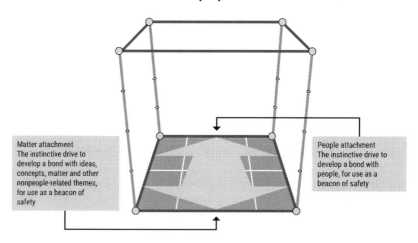

Matter attachment
The instinctive drive to develop a bond with ideas, concepts, matter and other nonpeople-related themes, for use as a beacon of safety

People attachment
The instinctive drive to develop a bond with people, for use as a beacon of safety

While our attachment style is deeply ingrained from an early age, the objects of our attachment – whether people or things – can change based on circumstances. Recognising and understanding your attachment style is crucial in both your personal and professional life. It informs how you interact with others, manage stress and approach tasks.

We want to reiterate that you can be effective in roles that don't naturally align with your attachment style, though it may require more effort and possibly lead to increased stress. Within limits that's okay – and might even help you to develop in your approach to complexity in maturity as we will see later. However, fundamental human psychology suggests that, as stress levels increase, you're more likely to revert to your innate preferences, setting aside learned behaviours.

Let's return to the Friday-night drinks scenario. Is the new colleague people or matter attached? At first you might think she's people attached, given that she first clings on to you, then looks for other people to talk to and enjoys their company. Yet, as she gets to grips with her new job and gets to know the company, your opinion of her might move along the attachment axis towards matter. At this point, we don't have enough information to place her on the attachment spectrum or assess how exploratory she is. This example simply illustrates the interdependence between attachment and exploration.

One common misconception is that individuals with a matter-attachment preference lack effective interpersonal skills. However, just as those who are people-attached can show a keen interest in technical subjects, matter-attached individuals can also display a profound interest in interpersonal dynamics – sometimes even pursuing careers centred around human interaction. For instance, psychotherapists, social-skills trainers and sales professionals often have a high degree of matter attachment. Sure, they work closely with *people*, but they usually take a technical approach to human beings. A psychotherapist, for example, might view a client as a system to be understood, whereas a salesperson might perceive a customer more as a complex set of emotions to be navigated. A matter-attached psychotherapist might be more intrigued by the intricacies of a patient's issues than by concern for the individual themselves. That's not necessarily a bad thing. In fact, it enables the psychotherapist to maintain a professional distance and prevents them from becoming overly involved in the patient's personal problems.

Similarly, people-attached individuals can have substantial technical expertise. However, their interest in 'matter' is often fuelled by their desire to engage with others. Their primary motivation lies in using their technical knowledge as a means to facilitate interaction with people. Their focus is on how a specific concept or theory can enhance or influence human interactions, rather than on the technical details for their own sake.

HOW TO NAVIGATE NETWORKING EVENTS AS A MATTER-ATTACHED PERSON

In our classes at the University of Amsterdam, we often discuss the dynamics of job-market networking. Typically, students with a matter-attached preference aren't very keen on events such as job fairs. Although they recognise the importance of meeting new people for their job search, they may not feel at ease in social settings. Their approach to networking can sometimes appear forced or awkward, which can be especially noticeable to people-attached individuals, who generally thrive in these environments and are naturally drawn to them.

If you're unaware that others may perceive you as socially awkward due to your natural matter-attached preference, you risk falling into a negative downward spiral. You feel uncomfortable at networking events, so you perceive them as unproductive, which makes you even more awkward... and your attendance at the event even less productive.

But wait! Maybe you have a secret advantage after all! Some of your people-attached peers are just too busy showing off their social skills. Perhaps they've forgotten that networking also has a matter-focused side. By understanding and embracing the event as a source of knowledge, you can transform the challenge into an opportunity.

One effective strategy is to leverage your natural strengths in preparation and research. Before attending a job fair, thoroughly research the companies and roles that most interest you. This will enable you to approach the event with a clear plan and a list of specific people to see. You may even pre-arrange some meetings. By setting up email appointments in advance, giving details about what you'd like to discuss, you can navigate the event more purposefully. By making the experience more structured, you can bring it into your comfort zone. Build on your natural inclinations towards structure and preparedness… and you might just turn a potentially vicious circle into a positive, upward spiral.

EXPLORATION EXPLAINED - IT'S ALL ABOUT THE INTRINSIC

Exploration can be defined as any activity aimed at gathering information about the environment. For the purposes of explaining the AEM-Cube, it's particularly helpful to distinguish between *extrinsic* and *intrinsic* exploration – a distinction that was first made by human behaviour experts, John Archer and Linda Birke.

Let's return to that Friday night in the bar and your new colleague, who by now is having a great time. In fact, so many people have bought her drinks that it's time to visit the bathroom. Her quest to locate it involves gathering specific environmental information to satisfy an immediate need. This is an example of extrinsic exploration – aimed at fulfilling a direct, personal need such as eating, drinking or social contact. It's a practical activity, focused on obtaining information for specific, often immediate purposes.

In contrast, *intrinsic* exploration is driven by a quest for change, especially when the familiar has become mundane. This type of exploration is not about meeting an immediate need but about a fundamental curiosity and a desire to seek out new experiences or ideas for their own sake. It's a pursuit of novelty and innovation, often without immediate practical application. This is the kind of exploration that defines our second axis of the AEM-Cube.

Let's go back to the bar near your office for one last time, just as your colleague is emerging from the bathroom. She scans the room once again and decides to approach a new group of faces, driven purely by the desire to meet as many people as she can. Finally, she feels safe enough to navigate the environment with confidence and is transitioning into a mode of completely intrinsic exploration. This shift reflects a fundamental human trait – a natural curiosity and a drive to discover the unknown, irrespective of immediate benefits.

The second axis of the AEM-Cube base is defined by a spectrum from stability-centred to exploratory-focused personalities. People at opposite ends of this spectrum have very different approaches to processing information and responding to their environment. Before diving into the details of what that means, we've listed some characteristics of both types of people. Do you recognise elements in yourself or close colleagues or friends?

Stability	Explorative
Think first, then speak. *Example: A project manager who carefully plans their response in meetings to ensure all factors are considered before deciding.*	Speak first, then think. *Example: A marketing executive who pitches a bold, untested advertising idea in a brainstorming session without fully considering the budget constraints.*
Aim to prevent problems. *Example: An IT professional who routinely updates systems to avoid potential security breaches.*	Address problems as they arise. *Example: An event planner who improvises solutions on the spot when unexpected issues occur during an event.*
Less inclined to initiate new ventures. *Example: A financial analyst who prefers to work with established models and techniques rather than experimenting with new methodologies.*	Frequently embark on new projects, sometimes without finishing them. *Example: A software developer who starts multiple app development projects, driven by excitement for new ideas, but struggles to complete them all.*
Value existing conditions and structures. *Example: A human resources manager who relies on time-tested protocols and procedures to manage employee relations.*	Draw energy from exploring new ideas and possibilities. *Example: A research scientist who thrives on developing innovative hypotheses and conducting experiments in uncharted areas of study.*

Embrace change cautiously, with a focus on minimising risks. *Example: A factory manager who carefully evaluates the options before expanding their product line, ensuring minimal risk to the existing business.*	Embrace change readily, sometimes without fully considering the consequences. *Example: An entrepreneur who quickly pivots their business strategy to capitalise on a new trend without thoroughly assessing its long-term viability.*

People process information in two primary ways: feedback-directed or feedforward-directed. Stability-centred individuals are feedback-directed, valuing control and tangibility, as they try to contribute to organisational stability. In contrast, those who are feedforward-directed focus on future goals, showing less concern for the existing situation and a greater eagerness for change. The differences are summed up in Exhibit 4.3.

Exhibit 4.3: The stability–exploration axis of the AEM-Cube

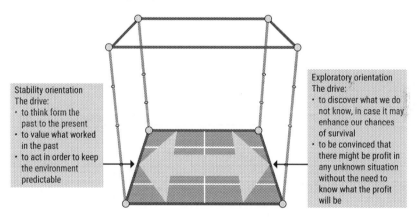

Stability orientation
The drive:
• to think form the past to the present
• to value what worked in the past
• to act in order to keep the environment predictable

Exploratory orientation
The drive:
• to discover what we do not know, in case it may enhance our chances of survival
• to be convinced that there might be profit in any unknown situation without the need to know what the profit will be

Individual preferences for exploration vary. Some people are comfortable within established structures and rules, finding satisfaction in refining and improving existing systems. Others are driven by a strong exploratory impulse, constantly pursuing new paths and experiences, undeterred by the risk of failure. They are the 'explorers of the new', as opposed to the 'conservers of the existing'.

THE TRAVELLERS: A TALE OF TWO PERSPECTIVES

One memorable incident in our classes involved a student whose AEM-Cube profile was highly explorative. She told us about her passion for global exploration and how she visited a new continent every summer holiday. As she described her adventures, the class listened intently.

Suddenly, another student raised her hand. 'I'm puzzled,' she said. 'According to my profile, I'm strongly stability-oriented and matter-attached, but I love to travel and visit new parts of the world too.' We asked for a bit more information, and she started to describe her past and future trips in meticulous detail. A clear picture emerged. Every minute of her journey was planned and booked well in advance – flights, trains, buses, hostels, restaurants and excursions. Nothing was left to chance or even last-minute changes of mind.

We then turned back to the first student: 'How about you? How do you prepare for your travels?' With a broad smile, she replied, 'Prepare?! I mostly go with the flow. I just buy a ticket, find a hotel when I arrive and let the adventure unfold.'

This exchange perfectly illustrates the spectrum of exploration within the AEM-Cube model. The first student, who thrives on spontaneity and the thrill of the unknown, embodies the exploratory end of the spectrum. In contrast, the second student, despite also being a world traveller, seeks comfort in thorough planning and predictability. She exemplifies the stability-oriented approach to life.

MATURITY IN COMPLEXITY: FROM THE FLOOR TO THE CEILING (THE M AXIS)

In our journey so far, we have travelled along the axes of attachment and exploration, which together define the floor of the AEM-Cube. These two dimensions provide a basic blueprint of personality traits. We now turn our attention to the third and more nuanced axis: maturity in complexity. This dimension sets the AEM-Cube apart from other personality models and was pivotal in our decision to incorporate the AEM-Cube into our course and this book.

Maturity in complexity is the ability to navigate and respect complexity, rather than avoiding paradoxes or simplifying situations into basic cause-and-effect relationships. It involves recognising the interdependencies of various factors in any situation and appreciating the bigger picture. In cybernetics, Ashby's Law of Requisite Variety states that for a controlling system to manage a complex situation effectively, it must have a level of complexity that matches the complexity of the situation. This is analogous to maturity in complexity. Think of it in terms of having the right tools for the job – the more tools (or internal complexity) a system has, the better it can manage different challenges.

Crucially, maturity in complexity differs from mere experience or talent. Someone might have considerable experience or be exceptionally skilled in a particular field yet struggle to effectively leverage these attributes, because they're unable to grasp the broader context of their environment.

It's also essential to understand that maturity in complexity is distinct from what we typically perceive as maturity based on age. While chronological maturity often conveys a sense of growing older and accumulating life experiences, maturity in complexity is about the depth and sophistication of understanding complex systems and relationships. It's about the cognitive and emotional capacity to navigate and manage intricate scenarios, which does not necessarily correlate with a person's age. For instance, a young professional might exhibit a high degree of maturity in complexity by demonstrating a strong ability to perceive interconnections and the consequences of their own actions within an organisation. Conversely, an older person might possess extensive life experience but still approach situations with a more simplistic, cause-and-effect mindset. All in all, you should view maturity in complexity as a specific dimension of personal and professional development, focusing on the ability to comprehend and manage complexity rather than chronological age or years of experience.

In the world of work, maturity in complexity is indispensable, particularly for leadership and management roles. Recognising and managing the intricate patterns of organisational dynamics and interpersonal relationships is all about maturity in complexity. Yet it's an attribute that's not limited to leaders. Any specialists who understand how their expertise contributes to the larger system in which they operate are likely to be more effective than someone who can't see the bigger picture.

In team dynamics, it's helpful to have a balance of maturity levels. Teams composed solely of members with high maturity in complexity might lack the spontaneity or speed necessary for certain tasks. Conversely, those with lower maturity levels can inject energy and drive into the team, even if they sometimes lack strategic foresight. In the end, though, it's the people with high maturity in complexity that are able to integrate diverse perspectives within a team. They're the team members who are adept at bridging gaps between different personalities, fostering a cohesive and productive working environment.

UNDERSTANDING MATURITY IN COMPLEXITY: FOUR STAGES OF DEVELOPMENT

Unlike the purely instinctive traits of exploration and attachment, maturity in complexity can develop and evolve through life experiences, self-awareness and self-management. Growth in this dimension often involves stepping outside of your comfort zone in terms of attachment and exploration. By recognising internal and external dynamics, reflecting on your actions and being receptive to feedback, you can increase your maturity in complexity.

In fact, the AEM-Cube defines four stages in the development of maturity in complexity, progressing from its floor to the ceiling (see Exhibit 4.4).

Exhibit 4.4: The four levels of maturity in complexity

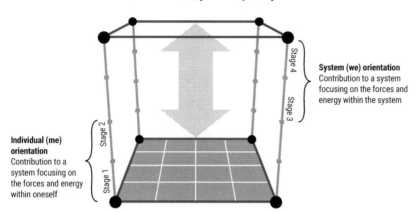

Stage 1: Developing self-awareness and reflective practice in professional growth

People at this stage often exhibit spontaneous and immediate reactions. Their spontaneity can be a double-edged sword. On the one hand, it fuels the generation of fresh ideas and injects a vibrant energy and creativity into their work, unencumbered by excessive deliberation. On the other hand, their unbridled enthusiasm and creativity can lead them to overlook broader organisational needs. Their approach sometimes results in a disconnect with the collaborative aspects of a work environment, causing them to operate in isolation. Recognising and balancing these aspects of your professional persona will be key to your effective professional development.

Stage 2: Dealing with your own professional competencies

In this stage, people demonstrate a more nuanced understanding of their professional environment, allowing them to shape their roles effectively and apply their expertise effectively within the organisational framework.

In stages 1 and 2, the focus is primarily on the "I" – personal growth, skill development and individual contributions, which directly relate to the concept of personal effectiveness we will discuss later. As we progress, however, the focus shifts noticeably from an individual-centric approach to a more collaborative, team-oriented perspective, which directly ties into organisational effectiveness – a concept we will introduce later. Stages 3 and 4 transcend the boundaries of personal achievement, steering us towards fostering connections with others and contributing to collective goals. In these higher stages, the emphasis pivots from the 'I' to the 'we', highlighting the importance of teamwork, interpersonal relationships and the synergistic benefits of working as a group. This shift underpins the evolution from personal accomplishment to collaborative success, reflecting deeper integration into the organisational ecosystem and a greater focus on shared objectives.

Stage 3: Working in a multidisciplinary manner

In Stage 3, the focus shifts significantly towards 'building bridges' within the professional environment and marks a transition from individual accomplishment to collective success. This stage is characterised by a deeper understanding of others' roles, functions and disciplines. At this point in their development, individuals become adept at connecting with colleagues across various domains, fostering a collaborative atmosphere. They start to think beyond their individual capabilities, asking key questions like, 'What does this team require in this particular situation?' and 'How can my unique strengths, and those of others, contribute to meeting the team's needs?'

Stage 4: Setting an example to others through consistent leadership

At this stage people have a heightened ability to perceive and understand the interconnections within their environment. Now fully mature in complexity, they comprehend how various segments within an organisation function and interact, recognising the distinct value each part contributes to the whole. As well as grasping the intricate web of relationships within an organisation, they understand its role and impact within a broader ecosystem. Leaders with a high degree of maturity in complexity are adept at valuing each team member's unique contributions. They skilfully integrate these diverse inputs into a cohesive and focused effort towards a shared objective. They're able to adapt their leadership style to suit various situations and consistently embody the values they advocate. In doing so, they set a standard for behaviour and culture within their teams or organisations.

One way of understanding the maturity in complexity axis is as a source of light on your 'comfort zone' within the AEM Cube landscape. The higher your position, the broader the pool of light on the floor of the cube (see Exhibit 4.5). As you grow more adept at managing complexity, you rise up the vertical axis and cast a wider circle of light, which allows you to step beyond your innate preferences smoothly and without stress.

Exhibit 4.5: Maturity in complexity as a beacon of light

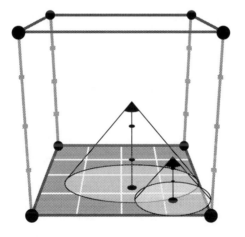

We'd like to emphasise that an elevated level of maturity in complexity doesn't signal the end of your developmental journey! Rather, it marks a stage where continuous growth and self-reflection become integral to your professional life. People at this stage are aware of their ongoing development and possess the self-awareness to continually reassess and adjust their perspectives and approaches. By the time they reach Stage 4, they have a deep understanding of the dynamic nature of personal and professional growth.

Developing maturity in complexity is not a linear process, nor is it the same for everyone. The path to maturity varies. If you're a strongly exploratory type of person, you may develop your maturity by actively seeking change, while your more stability-centred friends may develop maturity in response to their experiences. The journey is unique to each individual and shaped by personal and professional aspirations.

We'd also like to emphasise that greater complexity in maturity doesn't always equate to higher value. As previously discussed, teams thrive when they include members at different stages of maturity. In fact, certain roles are best filled by people who have *less* maturity in complexity.

In summary, maturity in complexity, as defined by the AEM-Cube framework, is about developing your ability to comprehend and handle complexity. It's a journey of personal growth that transcends basic experience or professional talent, focusing on the integration and application of your innate qualities, experiences and knowledge in the complex environment of the real world.

USING THE AEM-CUBE MODEL IN THE REAL WORLD

The following real-life example highlights the necessity of not only considering the content of your studies but also thinking about how you can apply your knowledge and skills in harmony with your personal strengths and the complexity of your environment.

Throughout our years of conducting careers classes, we have encountered a diverse mix of students. However, our very first group was an exception, consisting solely of 24 students of econometrics (statistical analysis of real-world economic data). We initially hypothesised that they'd all exhibit a high degree of matter attachment, with varying positions on the stability–exploratory axis and low to medium maturity in complexity. Surprisingly, one student deviated significantly from this pattern. She was strongly people-attached, positioned midway on the stability–exploratory axis, and scored exceptionally high on the maturity in complexity axis.

After the session, she approached us, visibly perplexed. She questioned everything from the accuracy of her AEM-Cube results to her choice of degree subject. Delving into her background, we discovered that her decision to study econometrics was heavily influenced by her parents, both econometrists. Despite finding the coursework manageable, largely thanks to her high IQ, she lacked a genuine passion for data and analysis. She often found herself working collaboratively, trading skillsets with peers who enjoyed the challenge of developing intricate computer models – a clear reflection of her high maturity in complexity.

Was econometrics the right field for her? We believed that it could be, depending on how she applied her knowledge. Given her people attachment and high maturity in complexity, traditional econometric roles like crunching data in a national statistical agency or designing algorithms seemed less suited to her. Instead, we suggested considering a career path that would capitalise on her subject expertise in a way that would meaningfully contribute to society. For instance, roles that involved translating statistical insights into societal benefits or communicating complex econometric concepts to non-specialists would align with her innate preferences for people attachment and her systemic perspective.

We very much doubt you're like our econometrics student. But that's the whole point of the AEM-Cube. Everyone has a different profile. The time has come to confront the ultimate real-life example: yourself.

APPLING THE AEM-CUBE TO YOURSELF

Having read this chapter carefully, some readers may have a rough idea of where they are positioned on the floor of the cube – as defined by their preference for matter attachment versus people attachment and their tendency towards stability versus exploration. They may also think they know which stage of complexity in maturity they've reached. Other readers may be less certain about where exactly they stand within the AEM-Cube. Either way, it's still worth going through a more formal and objective process of evaluation. People are often surprised by the results that come back from their AEM-Cube test. Even those whose image of themselves is confirmed may find their results reassuring. After all, it's essential to have an accurate picture before you start projecting yourself onto the many possibilities of the job market.

This is why we've included an exclusive online AEM-Cube test with this book. You can use the QR code on page 202 to access it. We suggest that you do this, *before* you read Chapter 5, where you will encounter the complex array of sectors, organisations and roles that constitute the working world.

CHAPTER 5
THE WORKING WORLD

Throughout our analysis of the dilemma faced by aspiring young professionals in the early chapters of this book, one fact was evident: it's impossible to decide how you would best fit into the job market if you don't know what the working world is or what it's asking for. Even once you've read Chapter 4 and completed the online assessment, it's still impossible to translate your newfound self-knowledge into a working environment that you don't know. Projecting yourself onto the working world is one of the hardest parts of the career-orientation process. It's also the reason that the well-meant advice, 'follow your passion, do something you like', is of little to no value.

This chapter is designed to give you an overview of what the working world has to offer. To help you make the link between yourself and the job market, the following pages paint a broad picture of the job market. Unlike the other chapters of this book, most of the information we present here is available elsewhere, perhaps in a more relevant or geographically specific form for you own needs (through your university's careers service, for example). So, do feel free to use other sources, especially for more detailed research. What's different about our approach, however, is that we advocate considering the working world from three different angles simultaneously:

- *Where* am I suited to working in terms of the sector or industry?
- *What* type of organisation would I best fit into?
- *What* role would I enjoy and be good at, within the sector and organisation?

For readers who like diagrams, this approach is summarised graphically in Exhibit 5.1.

Exhibit 5.1: The 'where' and the 'what' of the working world

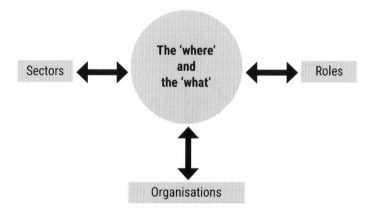

The most common approach to surveying the job market is by **sector or industry**. Most careers experts suggest starting by figuring out whether you want to work in government, consumer goods, services, financial services, technology and communications or healthcare, etc. The main problem here is that the choice is vaster than you might think! Industries like construction or automotive manufacturing don't just need specialist skills like architecture and quantity surveying or engineering and product design. They also need people with business skills like marketing, human resources and accountancy – many of which may not require any specific degree background or professional qualifications, at least to start with. Training in these functions is often 'on the job', with additional qualifications gained through professional bodies – and skills that are transferable to other sectors later in your career.

This takes us on to the concept of **roles**, which of course, are also a key consideration in traditional careers advice. Here, the main problem for first-time jobseekers is misconception. Job titles can be very confusing and not at all consistent across organisations! What does a 'brand manager' or a 'sales executive' actually do? (Quick answer: it depends!) What does a 'manager' do all day anyway? (Unhelpful answer: some manage teams; others manage projects or processes; most do a bit of both, as well as some additional work of their own! And being a manager in a research institute is very different from being a manager in a call centre.) Is a 'director' or a 'vice-president' more senior? (Even more unhelpful answer: it depends again... and anyway, it's probably too soon to be thinking about such senior positions.)

Quite often, when for instance a sports club is looking for a treasurer, they think that a person with banking experience is a good choice; he or she understands finance. But you should also ask yourself: what does he or she do at the bank? A controller's role would be relevant, while a commercial role would be less relevant.

So far, so traditional, in terms of careers advice. However, we believe that simply selecting a sector and a role isn't enough for a perfect career match. For a truly informed decision, you also have to take into account the nature of the **organisation** that you will be working for. As well as the economic activity of the organisation, you also have to consider its key characteristics: size, culture, ownership and stage of development. The size of an organisation will affect how much impact you can make on it. The culture will determine your daily stress levels. Culture is also linked to ownership. A company recently purchased by a private-equity firm is likely to be much more demanding than a friendly family-owned company, for example. And a start-up will be a very different working environment from a well-established company with many systems and structures in place.

The rest of this chapter consists of a whistlestop tour of the working world: its sectors, its organisations and its roles. We hope that reading it will provide answers about your preferences and priorities, as well as the reasons why you want to work. Of course, it is merely a summary and can't tell you everything you need to know. But simply getting more insight into what possibilities are out there is an essential stage in navigating your career.

THE SECTORS OF THE WORKING WORLD

The overview below (visualised in Exhibit 5.2) is a summary of the sectors that make up today's job market, in no particular order. For the sake of completeness, we felt we had to include this in the book, rather than consigning it to an appendix, but we realise the shortcomings of the descriptions that follow. For some people, there won't be enough information about the sectors that interest them; for others, there will be too much detail about industries they know they don't want to work in. We therefore recommend that you treat the following pages as a starting point for further research and skim over the sectors that hold no appeal.

Strangely (given what we said about the history of work in Chapter 2), the subdivision of the economic landscape into sectors is much the same as it was 50 years ago (except perhaps for the addition of Technology and Communication). But the experience of working in each of these industries has been transformed as a result of economic, social, political, environmental and technical trends. In fact, every single one of the sectors listed below is currently undergoing substantial changes as a result of digitalisation, especially AI, and the quest for sustainability in all its forms: environmental, social, ethical. Shifting regulations are also a major factor in many sectors. And who knows what global forces for change the future will bring?

Remember, the objective of this chapter is not to give you detailed insight into every sector. It is more aimed at giving you an overview of what the main sectors involve. As we mentioned earlier, most sectors have core activities for which specialist academic and/or professional qualifications may be required. Architects and structural engineers (in construction), and doctors, nurses and research scientists (in healthcare) are just a few examples. But in other fields, such as law or

Exhibit 5.2: The main sectors of the working world

Consumer	Automotive, Transport and Defense Mfg.	Construction
Services	Financial Services	Public Sector
Technology and Communications	Life Sciences	Energy and Power
Natural Resources	Materials and Waste Management	Capital Goods
	Third Sector	

software engineering, it may be possible to do a 'conversion' course. And many business roles (such as marketing, HR and accounting) may be open to anyone with the right basic qualifications and a desire to learn.

CONSUMER PRODUCTS

Let's start our tour in your local shopping centre, where thousands of consumer products are on sale. The sector encompasses a wide array of companies involved in manufacturing, distributing and retailing goods meant for personal use and consumption (whether basic or luxury or somewhere in between). In recent years, big data and social media, have been transforming market practices, while e-commerce is reshaping the entire sector. In fact, there may be a few empty shops in the imaginary mall you're standing in right now. Key subsectors include:

- Food and beverage – where hot topics include nutrition and sustainable packaging;

- Personal care and household products – from toiletries and cosmetics to cleaning materials and furniture – with a lot of rigorous research and regulation behind the scenes;
- Apparel and footwear – from design to manufacture and retailing, where the conflict between responding to trends and remaining sustainable is difficult to resolve.

Large household-name consumer products companies (like Unilever, Mars and Coca-Cola) and retailers (like Zara, Aldi and Decathlon) traditionally recruit big numbers of aspiring professionals in all business fields, as well as to technical or creative roles. These organisations can be great places to learn and to progress.

AUTOMOTIVE, TRANSPORT AND DEFENCE MANUFACTURING

Now let's leave the shopping centre and move out onto the street, where some much larger 'products' are in evidence: cars, motorcycles, buses and trams. Maybe you can also hear the distant rumble of a train, the metro deep below you or a plane high above. If you're near the water, you might be able to glimpse a ship or a boat. We hope, for your sake, that you can't hear the roar of a military jet or the whine of an attack drone (unless they're just on exercises) or any other defence equipment.

The sector that manufactures and supplies these products – and their millions of components – employs many, many young professionals. This is an industry made up of large and complex or small and specialist companies with commercial and management roles of all kinds, as well as engineering and technical career paths. They're interesting businesses to work in because they can be very competitive, cost-conscious and fast moving in some ways (think about 'just in time' manufacturing). However, they can be slow moving in others (imagine how long it takes to design a car and devise the production and supply chains to take it to market). There is also a heavy burden of safety and environmental compliance.

Recently, the advance of electric vehicles (EVs) and drone defence technology has been shaking up a sector that had been focusing on incremental improvements in design and manufacture for decades. In addition, artificial intelligence (AI) is already helping us to drive and park our cars, even if it hasn't taken over from humans to the extent that we may have expected. There are even more exciting times ahead!

CONSTRUCTION

Now, turn around and look back at the shopping centre itself. Then lower your gaze to the road or pavement you're standing on. Peer more closely, and you might see a drain cover, entrance to the sewers that carry away our wastewater or a fire hydrant connected to the freshwater system, with its pipes, reservoirs and dams. Next, start walking. Perhaps you'll walk across a bridge or through an underpass. On your way, you might come across a sign pointing you to the railway station, the metro, the airport the motorway, an industrial estate or a factory on the edge of town. We have all these jigsaw pieces of civilisation – not to mention our homes, places of study and places of work – thanks to the construction industry.

The most visible people in this industry are the skilled workers and unskilled labourers of many small, local subcontractors. But some of those men and women in hard hats may be wearing suits under their high-viz vests and working for one of much larger contractors, consulting engineers, architectural practices or maybe client company (or government agency). For a large construction or renovation project, the client usually appoints an architect and/or consultant for the design phase, as well as a main contractor to do the subcontracting and oversee the work. Again, there are many business opportunities (in sales, HR and accounting) as well as specialist careers (like structural engineering or construction management).

The rise of sustainability as a societal concern is adding another dimension to an industry that has always been focused on the environment (in both positive and negative ways). New technologies, materials and changing tastes are also a source of permanent change in a sector offering jobs that have always had a huge and visible impact on the world.

SERVICES

Almost as visible as products, buildings and structures (but sometimes a lot less tangible) are the consumer services we use every day. On the street outside the shopping mall, you see news-stands, cinemas and restaurants, all physical manifestations of the service industry:

- Media in the traditional forms of radio, television, film and publishing (books, newspapers and magazines), which have rapidly lost ground to social media, online gaming and on-demand streaming services throughout the 21st century. The most creative roles in the media are highly prized — and consequently, by the laws of supply and demand, tend to offer low starting salaries! Worse, AI is revealing new threats to many of the most sought-after jobs, such as journalism and acting.
- Entertainment in the form of cultural, musical and sports activities, as well as venues like cinemas, theatres, sports arenas, theme parks and zoos.
- Hospitality in the form of hotels, resorts, restaurants and catering. Trends include increasingly sophisticated pricing to balance capacity with demand.
- Travel and transport via rail, road, air, sea and underground services — all of which are highly regulated and require huge investment in infrastructure and equipment.

Transport also covers services like freight, shipping, logistics and courier services, which are mainly used by companies. This brings us into the more hidden world of business-to-business services (B2B for short). Other examples include:

- General services, such as temping, security, cleaning and recruitment agencies, usually based on well-defined and low-skill tasks — and driven by cost concerns. Robotisation is a threat to many of these jobs, but an opportunity for more senior professionals and managers in the industry.

- Specialist services – spanning everything from market research and editing to engineering and R&D, generally requiring high levels of skill and low levels of capital investment.
- Professional services: consulting companies, law practices, accountancy/audit firms, advertising agencies, real estate services, executive search... and more. Some of these organisations recruit a lot of graduates to high-paying roles and market themselves prominently on university campuses as potential employers.

In short, services are so diverse that it's impossible to generalise about working in them... except that they all involve engaging with people in some way, whether it's using a unique expertise to satisfy the customer or simply organising and running the service in an efficient, customer-friendly manner.

FINANCIAL SERVICES

One type of services is so vast, so distinctive and so hungry for young professional talent, that it deserves a description all of its own. These days, you're more likely to encounter such businesses online, rather than on the high street, but if you look carefully from your vantage point outside the imaginary shopping centre, you'll probably see a bank or two – or in the distance a high-rise office block with the logo of an insurance company in large letters.

Business-to-consumer (B2C) financial services like banking, insurance, investments, loans, mortgages, payments, pensions, currency exchange and more are embedded in daily life, whether we like them or not. Using them is a rite of passage to adulthood – and a source of employment for many young adults. Less visible is the provision of all these services to business. Among these providers are the investment banks that have become a source of high-paying, high-status jobs for young professionals over the last half-century or so, incorporating activities such as trading on the financial markets, corporate finance, initial public offerings, financial restructuring, mergers and acquisitions and research/analysis.

Investment banks have themselves become eclipsed by newer parts of the sector, like venture capital, private equity and hedge funds, although these tend to recruit people who already have some experience. And now, so-called fintech companies have disrupted the entire industry all over again! These innovators and start-ups, some of which have already turned into global giants, are reshaping all parts of the sector, especially B2C, integrating diverse financial services into seamless, consumer-oriented platforms (reminiscent of the one-stop-shop apps seen in China).

Other recent developments such as cryptocurrency (based on blockchain technology) are more controversial – and only go to demonstrate how hard it is for regulators to keep up with change in financial services... which takes us to the public sector, where those regulators work.

PUBLIC SECTOR

Services delivered by the public sector are even more diverse than those provided by the private sector but are similarly focused on supporting the customer, whether individual citizens or society in general. From where you're standing, on the street outside the shopping mall, you probably think you can't see much evidence of the public sector, unless you happen to be somewhere near the townhall. But turn around and look at your own reflection in a shop window. You are to some extent a product of public services. You were probably born in a state-regulated (if not state-owned) hospital, educated in state-regulated (if not state-run) schools and arrived here on a public transport or road system. What's more, you'd soon notice a world *without* public services. There would be rubbish piled up in the street and looters in the shops.

In most countries, the public sector recruits huge numbers of young people from a wide range of educational backgrounds into essential services like social work, housing, infrastructure welfare public safety, regulatory functions, policy formulation and administration. Education – from early years to university level – tends to be one of the largest employers of graduates. Although some educational organisations are privately run, they are always state regulated in some way. Likewise, healthcare, another huge recruiter of young talent (which we'll return to under the heading of 'life sciences' below). Depending on the country the armed forces, prison services and police may also have special programmes for entrants with degrees. Although salaries tend to be lower than in the private sector (and the work often subject to frustrating political interference and cost-cutting), the public sector remains attractive to young professionals with a strong desire to serve society.

Beyond this idea of doing public good, it's almost impossible to generalise about the public sector, not least because different countries do things in different ways. Local and national government, along with government agencies, are organised differently from country to country (with varying levels of private-sector involvement too).

What we can say, however, is that many areas of the sector are undergoing profound transformation, driven by digitalisation, data analytics and technology integration, all of which are being used to optimise service delivery, operational efficiency and transparency. From open data and e-government platforms to smart cities, technology is transforming the way we all interact with the state – and the work of young professionals employed by in the public sector.

TECHNOLOGY AND TELECOMMUNICATIONS

At this point we really need to say something about tech itself – the engine of economic growth for our times and the enabler of modern life as we know it. Over the past century, tech has revolutionised every other sector in our whirlwind tour of the working world and our individual experiences. Again, you won't necessarily see much evidence of technology out here on our imaginary town street, apart from maybe the empty shops rendered obsolete by e-commerce and the occasional 'smart' bus stop, with a video screen full of adverts on the side. Look instead inside your own pocket, at the smartphone on which your entire life depends.

It's hard to believe that at the turn of the millennium there were no smartphones, no social media and no streaming services. Cloud computing and big data were in their infancy, while AI was still the stuff of science fiction. Of course, there are downsides: cyberbullying and cybersecurity threats are just two negative consequences. And the recent pandemic revealed some strangely old-fashioned problems, for example in the supply chain for semi-conductors. However, the solutions usually involve further tech innovation and are thus the source of further economic growth and employment opportunities. It's hard to pin down and categorise such a rapidly evolving sector but here goes:

- Information technology (IT) includes the development and deployment of computer hardware, software and services. It includes software development, systems integration, IT consulting and cybersecurity services.
- Telecommunications covers the provision of communication services such as Internet, voice and data transmission – with infrastructure from cables under the sea to satellites in space.
- Consumer electronics focuses on the design, manufacturing and distribution of electronic devices such as smartphones, tablets, computers and smart home devices linked by the Internet of Things (IoT).

LIFE SCIENCES

Let's move from tech to *bio*tech and the rest of the life sciences sector. Here in the town centre, you probably can't see much evidence of it, except perhaps the odd pharmacy or optician's shop. Again, it's time to look deep within yourself and your past! Even if you've always been healthy, those antibodies in your bloodstream are there thanks to vaccines. And it's unlikely that you've never taken a painkiller or an allergy pill, visited a dentist or had an eye test. We hope, for your sake, that the life sciences industry hasn't been a big part of your life so far... but perhaps the sector, one of the largest recruiters of graduates, is part of your future?

Cutting-edge research, innovation and human ingenuity lie at the heart of life sciences – just like tech. But *unlike* tech, the research and development (R&D) process for new drugs, vaccines, therapies and medical devices can span years or even decades before there is a regulator-approved product. And many innovations come to a frustrating dead end. Once a new pharma product is on the market, drug companies have only 20 years or so to recoup their R&D costs, before their patent expires and so-called 'generics' can be produced at a fraction of the price. The operational landscape of life sciences is dominated by these cycles and broadly looks like this:

- Fundamental research, usually in universities or specialist research establishments;
- Biopharmaceuticals and drug development, focusing on the discovery, development and commercialisation of products to rigorous scientific and regulatory standards;
- Biotech and medical devices at the cutting-edge intersection of biology, engineering and healthcare – and increasingly involving AI;
- Healthcare providers and services, such as hospitals, clinics, dentistry practices, optometry services and specialist nursing homes (intersecting with the public sector in some cases).

Partly thanks to Covid-19, the world has woken up to the army of scientists, lab technicians and business specialists working across pharma companies, manufacturers, distributors, biotech start-ups, research institutes and universities – most of whom are driven by the desire to save and enhance lives. Since the pandemic, life sciences are cool again!

ENERGY

Another largely invisible industry that has been given a makeover by a global challenge is energy. With the possible exception of exploration and trading, coal, oil and gas have traditionally been seen as dirty and even dangerous industries, at least in the upstream parts of the sector (extraction and production). Meanwhile, the downstream parts of the industry (supply) were 'just another business'.

Then came the climate crisis, which turned companies in the sector into outright villains in the eyes of many members of Gen Y and Z! Some not only shun jobs in the sector but call on their universities to divest from it. A few even demonstrate at oil refineries. Meanwhile others choose to reshape the industry from within and accelerate the energy transition by working in this field for the traditional giants of the sector, like Shell and BP.

At the same time, the rise of renewable energy has created many new and smaller organisations, all keen to attract young talent. Solar, wind, hydro and battery technology are likewise hugely attractive to young professionals who want to save the planet. With many technologies still at an early stage of development, they're also exhilarating places to work, especially if you have a relevant degree. What's more, the energy transition has also cast the power industry, with its traditional utilities, infrastructure and associated technology in a new light. Grid modernisation and conversion to renewable supply are suddenly exciting and worthwhile areas to work.

Most parts of the sector rely on large-scale and long-term investment cycles, which make them interesting, if challenging, businesses to join. Energy is also heavily state-regulated and -taxed, which can be a further professional challenge. The recent outbreak of war in Ukraine and subsequent sanctions revealed just how dependent we still are on oil and gas – and how the price of oil affects costs and/or prices in every single one of the sectors described above and below. In short, to work in the energy sector, is to make an impact on everything! You may not be able to see the components of the energy business from where you're standing outside our imaginary shopping centre. But if there was a sudden power outage, the payment, stock-control, heating and lighting systems in each of those shops would fail, and they'd all have to close until the problem was solved.

NATURAL RESOURCES

Fossil fuels and renewables are not the only natural resources that we rely on every day. But unlike fuels, we rarely think about where these other natural resources come from or the potential harm that they might cause. Indeed, crude oil is itself the ultimate source of plastics, fabrics, fertilisers and many items that we take for granted. Most of the items for sale in the shopping centre behind you are derived from natural resources. So are the clothes you're wearing to go shopping. The sector covers much, much more, however.

- Agriculture doesn't just power the food chain. These days it also drives cars and trucks, thanks to biofuel production. And for centuries, it's supplied raw materials for pharmaceutical products and textiles such as cotton and linen. Employers range from tiny organic cooperatives to vast, mechanised prairie-style farms growing genetically modified crops.
- Forestry supplies us with pulp to make paper, timber to make furniture and fibres to make textiles. Moreover, trees are both a source of fossil fuel (firewood) and currently the only available large-scale carbon-sequestration technology.
- Mining is the extraction of mineral/metal ore and coal to supply the global economy (including the rare-earth elements on which much modern technology depends). While essential to modern life, mining raises concerns about pollution, water usage, land disturbance and human rights.
- Fishing is not just about heroic little trawlers but also involves huge factory ships out at sea, as well as fish/seafood farming offshore and inland. Sustainability of stocks and food safety are topical concerns.

As was the case for the B2B services we saw earlier in this chapter, most of the companies in this sector don't supply their products directly to the shoppers in our imaginary mall. But they do supply interesting and essential careers.

MATERIALS AND WASTE MANAGEMENT

This is the sector that processes many of the natural resources described above into useable commodities and raw ingredients for the consumer goods, construction, automotive, technology and life sciences sectors. Outputs include: chemicals, industrial gases, fertilisers, wood-based products, metals, paper, cardboard, plastics, glass and complex packaging. Again, the items in this chapter's shopping centre, not to mention the shops themselves, could not exist without these materials. Nor could the mall – or the rest of the modern world – function without an efficient waste management.

This brings us to the other face of the sector: environmental services and waste management. These companies dispose of and recycle hazardous and non-hazardous materials and wastewater, guided by regulations and public health considerations, including the need to send as little as possible to landfill.

Neither side of this industry is glamorous, but both prize professional skills, both technical and business. The rise of the circular economy and more sustainable industrial processes have given the sector a new dynamism and relevance. The rapidly changing regulatory landscape and constantly fluctuating raw- and recycled-material prices also make it a fast-paced environment to work in.

CAPITAL GOODS

An even more hidden part of the job market is the industry that makes the machinery, mechanical or electrical components used to manufacture and process everything else, as well as basic elements of infrastructure. It's possibly the most hidden of all the B2B sectors, but it's the engine of industrial progress, where professionals can make a real difference to the world by facilitating technological advance and sustainability. Automation, digitalisation and nanotechnology are key trends requiring specialist skills and business ingenuity. The companies involved may not be household names (although you may have heard of players like Schneider Electric, 3M and General Electric), but they play a part in producing every item in your house – and our imaginary shopping centre. Some are multibillion-dollar global businesses that touch every aspect of our lives and offer great early career opportunities.

THIRD SECTOR

These days, it's too simplistic to see the job market in terms of only public and private sector. Many graduates go straight to work for non-profits: from local charities to household-name NGOs, museums and international UN agencies. The so-called 'third sector' also includes not-for-profit social enterprises, grant-awarding foundations, specialist research institutes and think thanks. Perhaps, as you stand on our imaginary street, contemplating your future, you may be approached by someone asking for a donation to such an organisation. You might even have been asked to make an optional contribution via your payment card when you paid for your shopping inside the imaginary mall.

One of the core skills in this sector is in indeed fundraising, for which no specialist qualifications are needed, but depending on the organisation, specialist environmental, art history, logistics, event management, scientific, educational or even business skills can be beneficial. Non-profits, by definition, don't have money to throw around for training or high salaries, so it can be a good idea to grow your skills, build your pension pot and pay off your mortgage by working in another sector first.

Alternatively, if you really want to contribute to society or grand global challenges, you don't have to be directly involved. By giving generously to the third sector and assiduously paying your taxes to benefit the public sector, you may be maximising your impact on the world by maximising your earning power in the private sector or one of the many other kinds of organisations described below.

Yes, we've reached the end of our whistlestop tour of the sectors of the working world. We hope you've enjoyed your ride. Our next destination is the vast variety of organisations that can be found across these sectors...

THE MANY ORGANISATIONS OF THE WORKING WORLD

Before we explore the various facets of organisations, it's essential to understand their origins and defining traits. At their core, organisations represent a collective commitment to a common goal: providing products or services that are too complex or inefficient for an individual to offer alone. These offerings can be driven by demand, where suppliers fill existing gaps in the market (for example, an easy-to-use smartphone for the elderly) or they can be supply-driven, where new technological products create demand that no one had ever imagined before (for example, the original iPhone). Whether serving the public cause (like a police force) or maximising profits (like a private-equity firm) good, collective organisation is crucial to meet the needs of society and its markets effectively.

Today, bringing a product to market involves a complex network of individual expertise and meticulously crafted protocols. Imagine how many people and companies it takes to produce and sell you a smartphone of any kind. However, the way organisations create value for customers and end users varies significantly. An energy provider requires sophisticated machinery, natural-resource management, skilled engineers and craftspeople, efficient logistics, and a robust sales and marketing team. Meanwhile, a law firm primarily needs a reputation that will attract both talented professionals and the right kind of customers. To find your place in the working world, you shouldn't just take into account an organisation's products and services; you should also look at how it operates to deliver those products and services – which will depend on its size, shareholders, complexity, culture, purpose and stage of development.

Consider Heineken and Procter & Gamble. Both are multinational companies in the consumer goods sector and are publicly traded. However, they differ in notable ways: Heineken is a Dutch company with a primary focus on a single product (beer) and has maintained a family-business feel. In contrast, Procter & Gamble is a company with a diverse product portfolio and a corporate culture shaped by its American roots. Let's take a closer look at the characteristics that differentiate organisations, beyond their products, services and sector of operation.

SIZE

Clearly, organisations come in all shapes and sizes. They range from two-person design agencies or garage start-ups to multi-billion-dollar, multinational companies or the UK National Health Service (Europe's largest employer). But what difference does size make to the people who work in an organisation?

Generally, larger organisations have to be well-organised, with established systems, procedures and methods. They often provide robust training, planned management development and a professional environment. In such an environment, you can expect to find a high level of expertise and professionalism among your colleagues (although not all large organisations adhere to the same standards). The main downside is that as a newcomer, your impact and responsibilities may be limited. Autonomy and risk-taking are often not immediately possible, and the culture may feel formal and sometimes bureaucratic.

As the size of the organisation reduces, so the dynamics shift. Smaller companies tend to be less formal and more entrepreneurial, offering greater freedom and responsibility. Learning here is often experiential or 'on the job', involving trial and error rather than structured training. The quality of colleagues can be mixed, ranging from highly inspirational individuals to people who fail to thrive in an unstructured environment with comparatively little supervision.

Boutiques, scale-ups and start-ups take this shift even further. In these types of organisations, specific expertise or innovative ideas are paramount, and the quality of your colleagues significantly outweighs organisational structure. If you choose to work in such a setting, your platform for development is less the organisational structure, the systems in place, courses and training; it is far more about the people you are going to work with.

OWNERSHIP

Most people don't consider who owns an organisation before joining it. However, ownership structure can significantly shape a work environment. Consider the diverse spectrum of possibilities: publicly owned entities (state, local or quasi-autonomous), not-for-profits (foundations, interest groups, NGOs), listed companies, private equity firms, informal investors, cooperatives, private or family-owned businesses, partnerships and those created thanks to crowdfunding.

Each ownership model brings its unique dynamics. Professional shareholders, such as institutional investors in listed companies and private equity firms, often set high expectations for returns on investment within a clear timeframe, creating a strong focus on financial performance for every employee. This environment is typically bolstered by financial incentive systems, demanding rigorous performance and fostering a high-pressure atmosphere, which many people find professionally rewarding.

In contrast, publicly owned and not-for-profit organisations pursue ambitious goals with a focus on purpose. These entities often prioritise careful processes and quality of service over financial performance, cultivating an environment that values thoroughness and societal impact over immediate financial returns. This isn't to say that money doesn't matter. On the contrary, cost pressures and the need to maximise the impact of scarce resources can create as much stress as the need to make a profit.

Informal investors, family-owned businesses and cooperatives represent another intriguing category. These organisations often emphasise long-term goals and foster connections based on common interests or personal relationships. For instance, farmers' cooperatives create mutual benefits, while family businesses and may prioritise loyalty and a supportive, community-focused culture. The atmosphere is often friendly, informal, flexible and understanding, while objectives may be long rather than short term.

Partnership structures, prevalent in professional services such as auditing, law, strategy consulting and executive search, offer a unique blend of high service standards with a less stringent focus on cost efficiency. Also common in the medical field, these organisations maintain high expectations of service quality, emphasising professional excellence and collaborative ownership.

From an employment perspective, the implications of ownership structure are profound, particularly with respect to organisational culture.

CULTURE

Culture is to groups what personality is to individuals. But organisational culture is notoriously difficult to pin down and define. It can be helpful to think in terms of opposites: entrepreneurial versus bureaucratic; demanding versus laissez-faire; results-driven versus people-driven; trust-based versus fear-based; passionate about the product versus passionate about the outcome; formal versus informal; and high ethical standards versus low ethical standards.

There's no right or wrong when it comes to your cultural preference. To pursue a PhD, you know it'll take you three to five years of painstaking, detailed work, involving well-defined processes and collaboration with other experts. It's a very different pace of working life, compared to an equities-trading floor or an entrepreneurial venture, where quick decision making is key.

If we surveyed our readers about their cultural preferences, we reckon the results would be predictable. Today, in most wealthy countries, aspiring young professionals tend to value a friendly, safe working environment. However, it's important not to overlook the benefits of a results-driven environment, particularly at the beginning of your career. While a tough and demanding setting – such as the trading floor of an investment bank or a classroom in an inner-city school – might seem daunting, it can significantly enhance your skills and provide valuable experience. Although such an environment may not be ideal for the long term, it can provide a solid foundation and foster growth that proves beneficial in various career stages.

The culture of any company is usually influenced by its historical origins and its current stage of development – which takes us to a final key characteristic of organisations, which you should consider in conjunction with your AEM-Cube profile: their maturity.

STAGE OF DEVELOPMENT

The maturity of an organisation fundamentally drives its operational dynamics and can reveal what it would be like to work there. Business experts often visualise the lifecycle stages of an organisation (or an industry, product, service or project) using a diagram called an 'S-Curve'. It's also helpful to think about organisational stage of development in terms of the four seasons of the year.

Spring: A phase of vibrancy and new beginnings, marked by high investment in innovation and upscaling with a focus on effectiveness.

Summer: A period of peak productivity and profitability, where focus shifts to efficiency, often at the cost of innovation.

Autumn: Marked by a gradual decline, this stage is often characterised by a loss of market share and a sense of denial. Companies may resort to reactive strategies such as downsizing or returning to core principles to stabilise.

Winter: Different from autumn's reactive tendencies, winter represents a period of deep introspection and a clear, pressing need for renewal. In this phase, the continued decline in profitability and diminishing market presence act as potent catalysts, driving profound reflection and strategic reassessment.

Handling the rhythm of growth and decline in companies involves strategic flexibility. Without intervention, the curve naturally follows a bell-shaped trajectory (see Exhibit 5.3). For some organisations or products this may take many decades to play out (the oil and gas industry for instance). For others it may be only a few years (think about the lifecycle of the average smartphone).

Exhibit 5.3: The S-curve linked to the seasons

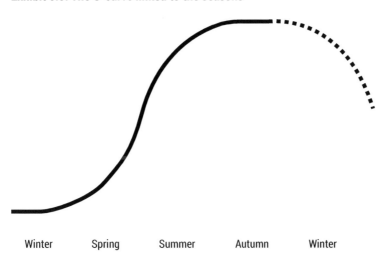

| Winter | Spring | Summer | Autumn | Winter |

The key to avoiding decline is to act during the 'summer', an opportunity that is often missed in the complacency that comes with success. To stave off decline, organisations can adopt one of two fundamental strategies: extending the existing curve or 'jumping' to a new curve (exhibit 5.4).

Extending the existing curve involves finding innovative ways to extract more value from the current business model or product. It's about enhancing and upgrading what already exists to prolong its relevance and appeal. A good example is the way Apple continually refreshes the iPhone by introducing new features – such as better camera lenses, enhanced screen resolution, sleeker design and faster processors. Each new model represents an incremental improvement over its predecessor.

While these enhancements are significant, they do not fundamentally change the product's core offering.

Jumping the curve is about redefining or radically altering the existing business model or exploring adjacent possibilities. It involves stepping into new territories or creating entirely different products or services. A good example of jumping the curve is Netflix's evolution. Originally a subscription based, mail-order DVD rental service, Netflix fundamentally altered its business model by transitioning into streaming services.

While extending the curve leverages and maximises the value of what already exists, jumping the curve requires a radical reimagining of the business to stay ahead of market trends and changes.

Exhibit 5.4: Two fundamental strategies to stave off decline.

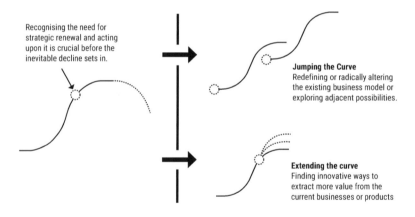

Recognising the need for strategic renewal and acting upon it is crucial before the inevitable decline sets in.

Jumping the Curve
Redefining or radically altering the existing business model or exploring adjacent possibilities.

Extending the curve
Finding innovative ways to extract more value from the current businesses or products

Perhaps you have already glimpsed the link to the exploration axis of the AEM-Cube profile. Stability-oriented individuals and teams, who excel in maintaining and improving existing structures, are typically more adept at extending the existing curve. They bring creative ideas to enhance current models or products. Conversely, those with an exploratory bent are naturally inclined towards generating ground-breaking ideas, making them more suited to situations where the focus is on jumping the curve

– regardless of their precise role within the organisation. And roles are our final destination in our tour of the working world...

ROLES

Job descriptions for various positions like consultant, online marketer and supply chain manager are readily available all over the Internet. However, understanding the core characteristics of these roles and how they fit into an organisation is even more important than listing the duties. What's more, given the proliferation of business jargon in the twenty-first century, it's far from easy to understand what any of these people do all day!

To add to the challenge, the rise of digitalisation has introduced many new job titles, such as 'search engine optimisation specialist', 'data scientist', 'machine learning engineer', 'cybersecurity specialist' and, perhaps most poetic of all, 'cloud architect'. These roles didn't exist 25 years ago. So, do the titles reflect entirely new functions, or are they modern iterations of past roles? The answer is likely both. While the specifics of these jobs may be new, their essence often aligns with the 'value chain' model created by the great American business guru, academic and writer, Michael Porter[12]. His breakdown of organisational roles (see Exhibit 5.5) remains relevant today.

In essence, whether you're drawn to a traditional role or a cutting-edge digital position, the fundamental functions within a company persist and have adapted to the evolving technological landscape. Understanding Porter's model will guide you in making informed career choices.

The value chain framework divides organisational activities into strategically relevant parts, distinguishing between primary and support activities. This distinction doesn't imply that primary activities are more important than support activities, but rather that they serve different functions. For example, a recruiter from HR (support) may be involved in the process of hiring a crucial new team member in operations, but

Exhibit 5.5: Porter's value chain model

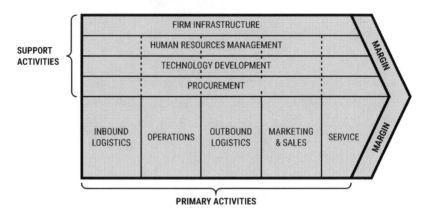

the final hiring decision rests with the operations manager (primary). Both roles are essential, and one cannot function effectively without the other. Similarly, there is no order of priority among the support activities.

Let's now delve a little deeper into Porter's model, relating different AEM-Cube profiles to each part of the value chain at the same time.

Although not specifically mentioned by Porter, regardless of the product or service, creation is the starting point – whether through fundamental research, technology development, market research or strategic vision. This innovative phase can involve breakthrough developments (like Apple's iPhone) or improvements to existing products (like Dyson's vacuum cleaners). Roles associated with 'creation' include technology, research and product development, essential in innovation-heavy industries like semiconductor manufacturing, but less so in fields like hospitality. Yet, even in the hospitality sector, businesses have to keep reinventing themselves in the long run, in order to stay in touch with shifting customer preferences. In the creative roles of any business, we find exploratory and content-oriented types to the fore, as new ideas and technologies (content) need to be devised before they can be implemented.

Once concretised, innovations need to be translated into components and processes in the supply chain, which encompasses procurement, operations and logistics, both inbound and outbound. This phase is about buying, making or assembling the product or service and preparing it for customer delivery, whether to consumers or businesses. This is also a content-heavy area but, in contrast to technological development, more suitable for less exploratory types. Optimisation takes precedence here over innovation.

However, both innovation and supply-chain optimisation are of little use if no one knows about the company's products or services. This is the domain of marketing and sales. While marketing professionals broadcast the selling points of the product to potential customers, sales teams target the most likely customers and close deals. Both marketing and sales consist of fairly exploratory roles, but marketing tends to be more content-oriented while sales is more people-oriented.

Marketing involves creating, communicating and delivering a so-called 'value proposition' to customers. Through market research, data analysis, branding, positioning and advertising, the marketing function supports sales professionals both in the short and long term. Traditional marketing roles include brand or product management, but digitalisation has introduced new positions like 'data scientists' and 'search engine optimisation specialists'. In industries like consumer goods, marketing is often seen as part of the primary process, a stepping stone to leading a business unit or even the entire company. Conversely, in financial services, marketing is considered a support activity, with product knowledge deemed more critical.

Sales isn't just about striking deals for monetary gain; even government policies must be 'sold' to gain public acceptance. Many people misunderstand the sales function, often associating it with aggressive tactics. However, selling varies significantly depending on the context and the organisational culture. More generally, consumer sales (e.g., retail, travel) is very different from business-to-business (B2B) sales, which requires deeper product knowledge and investment in long-term relationships.

Finally, at the end of the primary-activities chain, we find 'service', which has grown in importance with the advance of digitalisation, in both the B2B and B2C environments. In the past, service was always part of the after-sales and maintenance process for products like machinery. But with the rise of online purchasing, new elements of service have emerged for consumers. Returns and 'track & trace' are two prime examples. Roles in these new areas of service are more like jobs in hospitality in that they involve making customers delighted with their experience.

The stabilising backbone of an organisation's primary activities is what Porter calls firm infrastructure, encompassing, among other activities, finance, legal and quality assurance. Finance can be divided into control and treasury. Control covers bookkeeping, accounting, audit systems, management information and investment proposals – ensuring both administrative accuracy and support for business decisions. Treasury manages the organisation's finances, including shareholder relations, bank interactions, refinancing, taxes, currency and cash flow. All of the roles in this part of the value chain lean towards content- and stability-orientation. Legal functions are also content- and stability-oriented, but with more of an emphasis on words than numbers. They vary greatly by size and type of organisation. It may make sense to have an in-house legal team or to rely on external law firms for advice.

Human Resources (HR) focuses on the people aspect of an organisation, but paradoxically includes significant administrative components like salary systems. Despite its content-oriented aspects, it is often more appealing to people-attached, stability-oriented recruits.

Information technology (IT), which is equivalent to Porter's 'technology development', has become crucial to all organisations, not only for maintaining infrastructure and cybersecurity but also for supporting and accelerating business processes. But there are other technology roles too, ranging from software development and innovation to bridging the gap between technology and business, such as data scientists. These tend to be content-oriented positions, but tech also needs experts with more of a people-orientation to help translate business needs and make applications user-friendly.

We acknowledge that our examples predominantly come from the business world, with less focus on roles in the non-profit or third sector. However, while job titles and organisational characteristics may differ, the essence of these roles − and the AEM-Cube profiles of the people who fill them − remains consistent. In the educational sector, the 'products' are research, publications and teaching. These too need to be marketed. A university that fails to get high rankings or papers in top journals will struggle to attract students or funding. The public sector, whether local or central government, also mirrors these dynamics. Whether in policy advice, legislation, infrastructure projects, security or healthcare, initiatives must be created, shaped and accepted by the public or governing bodies, such as parliaments or municipal councils. In the medical field, similarities can be drawn with the hospitality industry, as both offer services to meet customer (or patient) needs. As well as specific medical expertise, there are many supporting roles, including managing patient flow (analogous to logistics) and aftercare.

Since Porter introduced his value chain model in the mid-1980s, technology has risen to prominence, not only for maintaining infrastructure and cybersecurity but also for supporting and accelerating business processes. In software, streaming and social media companies, whose products are entirely digital, inbound and outbound logistics as well as procurement have become almost non-existent, while technology development and operations have become almost indistinguishable. Similarly, with the arrival of social media and proliferation of niche marketing channels, it's questionable whether all marketing roles are truly part of the primary activity!

Nevertheless, after four decades, Porter's model remains a useful starting point for thinking about the value creation process and where you (and your AEM-Cube profile) might fit into it.

SEEING YOURSELF IN A SECTOR, ORGANISATION OR ROLE

We'll leave you to ponder your newfound insights into sectors, organisations and roles. No doubt, as you were reading, some appealed to you more than others. The main point to consider is that your reflections on this chapter should not stand alone. You have to align them with the reasons why *you* wish to work (Chapter 3) and your *own* self-awareness and innate preferences (Chapter 4). These connections will define the path you should be contemplating as you take your first tentative steps in the working world. In Chapter 6, we will dive more deeply into the different AEM-Cube profiles (including your own) and the type of roles that go with them. Who knows? You may find a perfect match.

CHAPTER 6
WHERE PERSONALITY
PROFILES MEET JOB ROLES

So far, in your quest to know yourself, you've explored the three distinct axes of the AEM-Cube – attachment, exploration and maturity in complexity, which we covered in Chapter 4. If you've completed the online assessment that accompanies this book (and possibly even if you haven't), you now also have a good idea of your position within the three-dimensional model.

In addition, in your quest to understand the job market, you've now gained an overview of the breadth of sectors, organisations and roles, as well as a general idea of how certain personality types fit with different kinds of environments and work. This is what we explored in Chapter 5.

Here, in Chapter 6, it's time to get more specific. We admit that this is a bit tricky for us. As authors, we have no idea about every individual reader's personal AEM-Cube profile. All we can do is recap on the possible outcomes of the test and begin to show how the four main personality types – as defined by positions on the floor of the AEM-Cube – might relate to different kinds of jobs. These are our modest objectives for this chapter.

For your part, the aim is simpler. It's to start matching your individual profile to some possible career opportunities. However, it will also be helpful to look at the other AEM personality profiles and associated roles. This will help you to understand what it takes to fulfil roles where you do not naturally thrive, which in turn will help you to increase your maturity in complexity and give you an idea of how different kinds of personalities can complement each other to create effective teams and organisations.

THE FOUR PRIMARY AEM-CUBE PERSONALITY PROFILES

First let's go back to AEM-Cube basics and look again at the floor of the cube. This is defined by the attachment axis (people attachment versus matter attachment) and the exploration axis (stability-centred versus exploration-centred). Although some people might sit right bang in the middle of one or both axes, most will fall into one of the four quadrants shown in Exhibit 6.1.

Exhibit 6.1: The four quadrants of the AEM-Cube floor

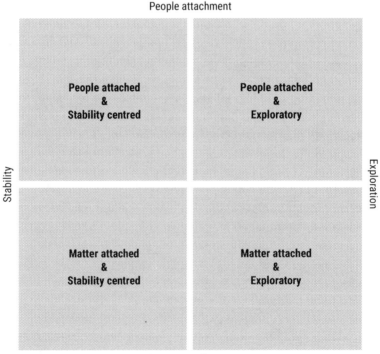

People attachment

People attached
&
Stability centred

People attached
&
Exploratory

Stability

Exploration

Matter attached
&
Stability centred

Matter attached
&
Exploratory

Matter attachment

Of course, everyone has their own unique combination of attachment and exploration preferences, but it's helpful to group these unique combinations into four broad personality profiles, each defined by one of the quadrants as follows (working clockwise from the top left).

- People-Attached & Stability-Centred: Individuals who value inter-personal connections and prefer a stable, predictable environment.
- People-Attached & Exploratory: Those who seek human interaction but are also drawn to novel experiences and change.
- Matter-Attached & Exploratory: People who are driven by content and ideas and thrive in dynamic, changing settings.
- Matter-Attached & Stability-Centred: Individuals who find comfort in tangible content and value consistency and structure.

Within each of these personality profiles, it's also possible to discern some key traits – as listed in Exhibit 6.2. Note that these descriptions are general and serve only as a rough guide. Each trait itself represents a spectrum. And individual human beings inevitably exhibit nuances that fall anywhere between mild to extreme expressions of the trait in question.

As you can probably guess from the words used to describe the traits (remarkably similar to those used in recruitment ads and job descriptions), understanding where you fall within these quadrants can be incredibly beneficial in the job market. If you can match your natural inclinations and strengths with corresponding roles in the world or work, you will have greater job satisfaction and perform more effectively.

The third dimension, the maturity-in-complexity axis, extends vertically from the foundational floor of the AEM-Cube, adding a critical layer of depth and nuance to the four basic personality profiles. By considering this third dimension, you'll gain a fuller picture of your individual capabilities and potential, allowing for an even more targeted and effective approach to the job market and its many different organisations.

Exhibit 6.2: The key traits of the four primary personality profiles

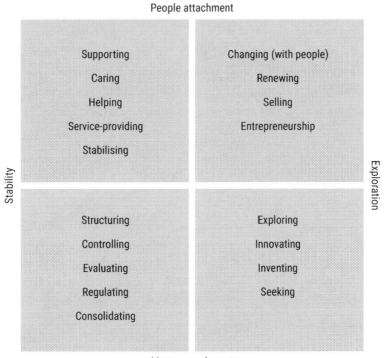

People attachment

Supporting	Changing (with people)
Caring	Renewing
Helping	Selling
Service-providing	Entrepreneurship
Stabilising	
Structuring	Exploring
Controlling	Innovating
Evaluating	Inventing
Regulating	Seeking
Consolidating	

Stability · Exploration

Matter attachment

We'll touch on maturity in complexity, as we continue delving into the each of the four primary AEM-Cube personality profiles in turn (summarised in Exhibit 6.3) and at the end of the chapter. For each of the four quadrants, we'll suggest job roles that typically align with the profile and examine potential challenges in collaboration. Remember, the following pages are meant to serve only as a general guide. In the real world, job titles can be deceptive and shouldn't be your sole criterion for decision making. You should thoroughly evaluate the specifics of each role you apply for, along with the responsibilities it entails. Above all, look beyond the nature of the work itself and the environment in which you'll be operating. One final tip: by all means, focus on your own quadrant, but – to improve (or satisfy) your maturity in complexity – read about the other personality profiles as well. You will learn how people with a different profile can add value by looking at world differently.

Exhibit 6.3: A summary of the four main personality profiles

People attachment

Sustainers	Prospectors
Caring, give attention, patient, sensitive to atmosphere, saviors, avoiding conflict.	Manifesting, steering, together with others, high EQ, connectors, participative
Need to learn to say "no"	Allergy to sustainers
Idealists Learning through people	Syntheticists Learning through practical and applicable ideas
Conceptualisers	Pioneers
Researching, procedural, critical, rational	Leading, discoverer, inventor, expert, rational.
Allergy to prospectors (conflict), frustration about pioneers	Frustration about sustainers. Suspicious about prospectors.
Functionalists Learning through real situations and ordering	Analysts Learning through research and analysis

Stability ← → Exploration

Matter attachment

THE SUSTAINERS: PEOPLE-ATTACHED / STABILITY-CENTRED

Characteristics

Individuals in this category thrive in nurturing roles, prioritising attention, care and support for others. They value a harmonious atmosphere and exhibit patience and a willingness to accommodate others. However, they may avoid conflict and suppress their own needs, which can lead to frustration or passive-aggressive behaviour. With maturity, they learn to balance their needs with those of others, improving their conflict-resolution skills.

Cooperating with others

Members of this category have few problems cooperating with other people. They often assume the role of 'saviour' and cover for others when things start to go wrong. Workmates like having them in a team. As they develop their maturity in complexity, they will learn to say 'no' to others and 'yes' to themselves more often.

Examples of roles where sustainers thrive
- Healthcare professions: roles like nursing, therapy, medical administration, where empathy and patient care are crucial.
- Customer service and support: roles that involve assisting customers before and after sales, addressing their concerns and ensuring a satisfactory experience.
- Human Resources: especially in roles focused on employee relations, benefits management and workplace wellness.
- Education and training: positions like teaching, academic advising or training coordination, where supporting and nurturing learners is key.
- Social work: roles that involve supporting and assisting individuals, families or communities in need.
- Hospitality and event planning: positions in hotel management, event coordination or customer relations, where creating a welcoming atmosphere is essential.
- Community outreach: roles that involve building and maintaining relationships with community members and stakeholders.
- Administrative and executive assistance: where organisational skills and the ability to maintain a smooth and efficient office environment are valued.
- Counselling and life coaching: providing guidance and support to individuals in personal or professional development.
- Public relations: roles that focus on maintaining a positive public image for a company or organisation.

THE PROSPECTORS: PEOPLE-ATTACHED / EXPLORATORY

Characteristics
Prospectors are driven by the need to engage with others and are sensitive to the dynamics of change. They can temporarily overlook content to focus on social relationships, facilitating a conducive environment for

achieving results. As their maturity in complexity develops, they become effective 'bridge builders', who use their people skills to unite teams. What they all have in common is that they are emotionally intelligent and can get others to commit to the organisation or a cause.

Cooperating with others

This personality type's greatest conflicts and irritations arise with people from the quadrant in the opposite corner of the AEM-Cube floor (matter-attached / stability-centred). Both sides often need an elevated level of maturity in complexity if they are to bridge the gap between them and accept that neither the one nor the other has a monopoly on success.

Examples of roles where prospectors thrive

- Project management: running diverse projects where coordinating team efforts and managing dynamic requirements are crucial.
- Human resources: roles focused on talent acquisition, employee engagement and organisational development, where understanding and motivating people is key.
- Marketing and public relations: roles that involve creative campaign development and building relationships with clients, media and the public.
- Event planning: coordinating events where attention to detail and the ability to manage changing circumstances are essential.
- Training and development: building and delivering training programmes with diverse learning styles and motivating participants.
- Community outreach and non-profit work: roles that involve building relationships with community members and stakeholders to drive social change.
- Sales and business development: positions that involve building new client relationships and exploring new market opportunities.
- Change management consultancy: advising organisations on managing change effectively, requiring an understanding of both the human and operational sides of change.
- Team leadership roles: especially in dynamic environments where leading by influence rather than authority is important.

- **Customer success management:** fostering long-term relationships with customers and ensuring their continued satisfaction and engagement with the product or service.

THE PIONEERS: MATTER-ATTACHED / EXPLORATORY

Characteristics
These creative thinkers are deeply involved in the content of their work, often driving innovation. They excel in environments that require the development of new ideas or participation in change. As leaders, they tend to focus more on content than on human interaction, which can be a double-edged sword, fostering a content-driven environment but potentially overlooking interpersonal dynamics.

Cooperating with others
Challenges may arise in collaborating with matter-attached, stability-centred individuals, who might find their creative process disruptive and their attention span for details and optimisation unsatisfactory.

Examples of roles where pioneers thrive
- Research and development (R&D): roles in departments where developing new products or services is key.
- Software development: particularly in roles focused on creating new software solutions or pioneering new technologies.
- Product design and development: involving creative design processes and innovative product creation.
- Strategy consulting: developing long-term strategies for organisations, which requires analytical and forward-thinking skills.
- Entrepreneurship: starting their own business or leading other people's start-ups, especially in the technology or creative sectors. Often the inventors of new business ideas... but not necessarily able to market their own concept!
- Data science and analytics: roles that require innovative approaches to interpreting data interpretation and solving problems.
- Engineering: especially in fields that are evolving rapidly or where innovative solutions are constantly required.

- Creative direction in advertising or marketing: overseeing creative processes and initiating innovative campaigns.
- Legal advice on technology or intellectual property: where understanding complex, evolving content is crucial.
- Financial analysis for innovative financial products: where innovative thinking is applied to financial models and market strategies.
- UX/UI design: creating innovative user experiences and interfaces for digital products.

THE CONCEPTUALISTS: MATTER-ATTACHED / STABILITY-CENTRED

Characteristics
People in this group prefer structure and procedures over abstract concepts. They excel in roles that require meticulous attention to detail and are likely to propose solutions to improve processes. Their strength lies in their ability to maintain and control established systems.

Cooperating with others
Matter-attached, stability-centred people can identify strongly with colleagues in the same profession and enjoy maintaining contacts with them. The greatest problems arise when they're cooperating with strongly exploratory people. A person who is matter-attached and stability-centred tends to raise objections to ideas suggested by an exploratory colleague. Such a person is also unafraid to point out weak points in a colleague's proposal. This means the exploratory person will often complain that a conceptualist is nit-picking, fault finding or, worse, putting the brakes on an exciting new project. The more maturity in complexity the conceptualist gains, the more they learn to use other people's strong points and their own to best advantage. From then on, they function as the 'supporting beam' of their team and organisation.

Examples of roles where conceptualists thrive
- Quality control and assurance: positions focused on maintaining and improving product quality through rigorous testing and adherence to standards.

- Legal professions, such as lawyers, paralegals or legal assistants, where attention to detail and procedural accuracy is essential.
- Accounting and finance: roles like accountants, auditors or treasurers, where precision in handling financial data is critical.
- Operations management: overseeing operational processes in manufacturing or production environments.
- Supply chain management: organising and optimising logistics, supply chain efficiency and adherence to operational protocols.
- Data analysis: roles involving the analysis of data sets, where precision and attention to detail are crucial.
- Technical writing and documentation: creating and maintaining detailed documentation, manuals and procedural guides.
- Risk management and compliance: ensuring organisational adherence to laws, regulations and internal policies.
- IT systems administration: managing and maintaining IT infrastructure and cyber security within established guidelines and procedures.
- Architectural and engineering technicians: assisting in the development of architectural or engineering plans, ensuring accuracy and compliance with industry standards.

THE ROLE OF MATURITY IN COMPLEXITY - THE VERTICAL AXIS

As we've already glimpsed, the maturity in complexity axis refines the four primary personality profiles by focusing on the *application* of innate preferences, moving along a spectrum (with four clear stages) from 'self-expressive' to 'integrative' behaviours. In other words, the vertical axis of the AEM-Cube adds another dimension to your personality profile by characterising your approach to your professional role. It plays a crucial role in the way you adapt to and perform within various work environments, effectively guiding you towards where you can best leverage your abilities and grow.

More self-expressive individuals (Stages 1 and 2) are better suited to roles emphasising personal effectiveness, where independent creativity and problem-solving are paramount. Examples include programmers, writers, coaches and scientists. People with a more integrative approach

(Stages 3 and 4) may work in a similar capacity, but they're more likely to excel in persuasive communication and compelling argument, whereas their self-expressive colleagues often find efficiency and autonomy to be their strong suit.

The strengths of more integrative individuals (Stages 3 and 4) lie in jobs requiring organisational effectiveness, where collective outcomes outweigh individual excellence. This personality type excels in roles that demand coordination, team synergy and a holistic perspective. Ideal positions might include leadership, project management and event planning, where the ability to integrate various elements in pursuit of a common goal is crucial. Self-expressive individuals in such roles find it easier to take decisions but might fail to hit collective goals. Integrative people, on the other hand, might take too long to take a decision. Remember, integrative people, can always see other people's points of view, even when these conflict, and might therefore struggle to find the right way forward.

TAILOR YOUR JOB-SEARCH STRATEGIES TO YOUR PERSONALITY PROFILE

If you've been paying attention throughout this chapter, you'll already have realised that there are no clear-cut correlations between personality types and ideal jobs. The reality is more nuanced, with job titles and classifications that can be misleading. HR stands for 'human resources', which sounds ideal for anyone who's strongly people-attached, but it includes managing payroll systems and writing technical job descriptions, which are more suited to matter-attached candidates. It's therefore crucial to scrutinise the actual role and expected tasks involved in any job you apply for. And remember, you *can* succeed in roles outside your natural attachment style, although it may require more energy.

The same goes for the organisations you decide to apply to. It turns out that many seemingly stability-focused employers like government agencies, healthcare institutions or utility companies host some highly exploratory roles. Consider a team in a utility company exploring renewable energy sources, for instance, or a policy researcher in the civil service. Conversely, start-ups, often seen as hubs for exploratory roles, may also need stability and matter-oriented individuals for functions like daily cash flow optimisation.

In short, the AEM-Cube is not a magic job chooser – like Harry Potter's 'sorting hat'. Instead, it's a tool to help you get started on the long, hard road of your job search. The good news is that, as well as helping you decide whether a job is right for you, it can also make the job-search process itself easier. We believe it's important to adopt a job-search strategy that aligns with your natural tendencies – which will ultimately enhance your chances of securing the right job. A tailored approach that plays to your innate strengths will make the process not only more intuitive but also more successful. By embracing a method that feels instinctive to you, you are likely to navigate the job market more effectively, leading to opportunities that are a better fit for your unique profile.

Matter-attached people, true to their nature, best approach the job market with a focus on content. They're likely to be more successful in identifying potential roles through targeted and structured methods. Sifting through job sites, monitoring the recruitment pages of companies that particularly interest them and setting up detailed Google Alerts or LinkedIn searches can be particularly effective strategies for them. On discovering a role that piques their interest, they can delve into more detailed research, both about the position and the organisation. This may involve reviewing online resources or reaching out to current employees with specific questions to gain deeper insights. Their approach to understanding a role and its fit within a company is likely to be meticulous: they will gather as much information as possible and analyse it all carefully. This comprehensive research will then inform their application process, allowing them to tailor their CV or online form precisely to the job's requirements and the company's culture. For a matter-attached candidate, a methodical and information-driven approach not only increases the likelihood of finding a suitable role but also prepares them for presenting themselves effectively in the application and interview stages.

For people-attached job seekers, the most natural approach to the employment market is inherently relational and interactive. These candidates often find greater success through networking and fostering connections. Rather than relying exclusively on online job portals or company recruitment pages, they flourish in more interactive settings like networking events, career fairs or professional gatherings. They may actively engage with current or former employees of their target companies on platforms like LinkedIn, or even initiate casual conversations over coffee. This approach not only helps them to understand the company culture and specifics of a role but also frequently uncovers job opportunities before they're advertised. Their primary focus lies in grasping the interpersonal dynamics within a work environment, in addition to the job responsibilities.

The application process for a people-attached person is again likely to be influenced by their personality characteristics. They use the information gathered from networking conversations to tailor their application, highlighting how their personal attributes and skills align with the team and organisational culture. Their natural inclination towards building relationships and understanding people dynamics equips them to present themselves as a candidate who fits not only the job requirements but also the social fabric of the organisation.

Regardless of whether your approach is people-attached or matter-attached, it's crucial to consider and prepare for encountering the opposite perspective at some point in the job-search process. When you engage with an interviewer from a different quadrant of the AEM-Cube floor, the interview may not align perfectly with your innate preferences. It's important to strike a balance. If you're matter-attached, you may naturally focus on the technical aspects of the role, but you should also try to understand and ask about the company culture. Conversely, if you're people-attached, while your inclination might be to emphasise interpersonal dynamics and company culture, it's equally important to show that you've thoroughly understood the specific job requirements and responsibilities.

In essence, a well-rounded approach that considers both the technical and cultural aspects of a role will prepare you for a broader range of interview styles and questions. This balanced understanding will ensure that you can effectively display not only how well you fit the role technically but also how well you align with the organisational environment and team dynamics. Comprehensive preparation will make you a more versatile and appealing candidate in any interview scenario.

THE AEM-CUBE AS AN INTERVIEW ASSET

Insight into your innate preferences can equip you with a more refined vocabulary for engaging with companies or recruiters. Often, early-career professionals find questions like 'Where do you see yourself in ten years' time?' challenging to answer. Understanding your profile can give you clarity and confidence in your responses. For instance, if you identify as a stability-centred, matter-attached person, your answer might be along the lines of:

> In ten years, I see myself in a role where I can make use of my deep focus and attention to detail in a structured environment. I'd like to grow into a position where my ability to work systematically and efficiently makes a more significant contribution to long-term organisational goals. Ideally, this would be in an area that allows me to develop and apply my specialist skills even further.

This response not only reflects your innate preferences but also communicates to employers your understanding of how your natural inclinations might align with potential roles and the value you can bring to a stable, detail-oriented work environment.

If you identify as exploratory-focused and people-oriented, your response to the question, 'Where do you see yourself in ten years' time?' might be:

> In ten years, I see myself thriving in a leadership role where I can channel my passion for innovation and collaboration. I hope

to be at the forefront of developing new ideas, working closely with a wide range of colleagues to turn these ideas into a reality. My goal is to be in a position where I can inspire and motivate others, fostering a creative and inclusive environment with lots of opportunities for learning. Ideally, this would be in an area that allows me to build on my natural strengths of teamwork, communication and adaptability.

This answer highlights your natural inclinations towards innovation, teamwork and leadership, demonstrating to recruiters your enthusiasm for roles that require adaptability, creativity and strong interpersonal skills.

Your journey through the job market is uniquely yours, and the AEM-Cube provides a framework to help you navigate it – guided by insights about *yourself*. Other personality tests may reveal other facets of your character, but the axes of the AEM-Cube are particularly relevant to the world of work: stability versus exploration; people versus matter attachment; and maturity in complexity. By aligning your job search with these innate tendencies, you enhance your chances of finding not just success but roles that offer genuine satisfaction and growth. The key to a fulfilling career, as we have already glimpsed – and will see more clearly in Chapter 8 – lies in understanding yourself and finding a workplace where your natural preferences are not only recognised but developed, celebrated and used to their fullest potential.

If you'd like to find out more about the AEM-Cube, we recommend reading Peter Robertson's book, *Always Change a Winning Team: Why Reinvention and Change are Prerequisites for Business Success.* It was instrumental in shaping the chapters in this book that discuss the AEM-Cube, along with insights from the authors' students, colleagues and personal experiences. But before you research the AEM-Cube in more depth, please carry on reading this book!

THE POWER - AND THE PUZZLE - OF SELF-KNOWLEDGE

By now you may be more bewildered than when you started to read Chapters 4, 5 and 6. We hope you have discovered that there are more opportunities in the world of work than you previously imagined – and many of them are a possible match for your profile. We understand how puzzling it can be. You thought you just had to decide which jobs to apply for... and now it seems you have a plethora of sectors, organisations and roles to choose between.

Fear not! In Chapter 8, we'll zoom in on the pressing and practical question of 'how to choose'. But first, we think it's important to understand *what* you're choosing. A career is much more than a random series of jobs. That's why we're devoting Chapter 7 to helping you understand the three phases of working life.

CHAPTER 7
THE THREE PHASES
OF WORKING LIFE

So far, we've analysed the job-market dilemma (Chapters 1 and 2), developed some self-awareness (Chapters 3 and 4), gained an overview of the working world (Chapter 5) and started to trace the connections between roles and personality types (Chapter 6). You'd be forgiven for thinking that you have all the information you need to make your first big career choice. But sorry, we're not quite there yet!

We fully understand that, as an ambitious young professional, you're primarily interested in what you are going to do in the next few months – and you're not too concerned what your longer-term future might hold. However, with so many options on the table, we recommend that you also understand their implications in terms of career development. Thinking about where you're heading *tomorrow* will help you to understand whether you've made the right career choice *today*, which is particularly important to people who like to measure their progress constantly (a typical trait of Gens Y and Z, we're told). Not only will looking ahead help you to make the right choice; it will also help you to answer those tricky interview questions about your future ambitions.

To illustrate the importance of looking ahead, consider the simple fact that very few people move seamlessly between the public and private sectors during their working lives. This isn't just because salaries are generally lower in the former; it's also because people in business don't fully understand what people paid in the government do – and vice versa. Similarly, people who start their working lives in small entrepreneurial start-ups may find it hard to adapt to the less dynamic, process-driven culture of large corporates. And graduates who make the apparently sensible choice of investing the first ten years of their career in a multinational household-name company or a prestigious consultancy might be viewed as 'too corporate' by an entrepreneur seeking to recruit a successor. In other words, your initial choice will probably have an impact on *all* your subsequent choices.

Let's take the story of Sue, who participated in our classes at the University of Amsterdam. An econometrist, she was incredibly smart and very keen to make a positive difference in the world. In fact, she was considering working for the charity, SOS Children's Villages, rather than joining the strategy consultancy that had offered her a job. That's when Sikko involved her in one of his famous thought experiments! 'Suppose we could clone you,' he said. 'Sue-1 joins SOS Children's Villages and Sue-2 joins a strategic consulting firm. After five years, an exciting new strategy role comes up within SOS Children's Villages. Both Sues apply for the job. But who is the best choice from the charity's point of view? Sue-1, who knows the organisation and all its operations from the inside? Or Sue-2, with her impeccable professional credentials, strategy expertise and external perspective – and whose passion for doing good is undimmed? There's no right answer, but the real, uncloned Sue decided to take the SOS Children's Villages job.

The examples and story above explain why Sikko is sharing his three-stage model of working life in this chapter. We also think the model is essential for fully understanding the relationship between career demands and personality types or natural preferences. The model, represented visually in Exhibit 7.1, is based on the metaphor of a house: building it and living in it but also the vital preparations for construction.

Exhibit 7.1: The three-stage model of working life

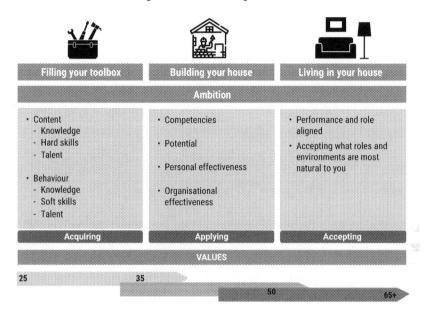

Roughly speaking, the first ten years of your working life is about filling your professional toolbox. You learn how to use a metaphorical hammer, saw and screwdriver. You also get an idea what building houses might involve – and what kind of house would suit you best. To pursue the metaphor, the second phase of working life is about using the tools in the box to build your house. This requires different kinds of expertise: bricklaying, plumbing, carpentry and electrics, all of which have to be organised and aligned. By the third phase, from the age of 50 or so, you are going to live in the house you have built – and hopefully flourish!

These three phases represent how a working life develops. First, during school, university and your initial working experiences, you learn and acquire knowledge and skills. Second, you apply what you have learned, ideally to obtain greater responsibilities and more senior roles – or perhaps to transfer your knowledge and skills to an entirely new context. Frequent job-hopping and even radical career change are, after all, very common these days. The third phase is not only about transitioning to your most senior roles; it's also, more importantly, about admitting and accepting who you are in relation to your natural preferences and capabilities. At this final stage, you shouldn't be aspiring to jobs or working environments that lie outside your natural preferences and the skillset you have spent a lifetime developing. It will benefit no one!

As well as explaining the metaphor in more detail, this chapter will also help you to answer some fundamental questions. How do I know what my potential is? How can I grow and develop? And what does it take for me to perform to the best of my ability?

PHASE 1: FILLING YOUR TOOLBOX

Acquiring a hammer, screwdriver and saw – and learning how to use them – may not appeal to members of Gens Y and Z, who would probably prefer to start building their house straight away. We admit that it sounds a bit old-fashioned, but believe us, a properly filled toolbox will always be beneficial and is a must if you're going to build a high-quality house. In career terms, filling your toolbox is about acquiring knowledge, developing skills and exploiting your talents, both from a 'content' and behavioural perspective.

To explain what we mean by **content**, knowledge can be about many different things: knowledge of what a role involves; knowledge about an organisation and its people; knowledge about an industry and its environment; knowledge about specific expertise and techniques; and specific product knowledge. Hard skills are a step up from knowledge because mastering them enables you to add value. They can relate to a specific business function (like marketing or IT), analytical methods (for example, the techniques used in strategy consulting or the calculations used to value a business) or a profession (such as medicine, law or carpentry). Some of these hard skills are easy to acquire; for others you need a certain talent. If you're not musical, it's unlikely that you'll become a successful pianist. If you have no ball sense, it's unlikely that a career as a professional footballer will be on the cards. If you have a feel for numbers, technical studies or working environments will probably suit you well.

On the **behavioural** side (which is correlated with the people-attachment dimension of the AEM-Cube), filling the toolbox is more about understanding when, how and in what situations to use which tools. Suppose you can use a screwdriver and a hammer (a hard skill), but you find yourself in a situation where you must choose whether to put in a screw or a nail. Or, in less metaphorical terms, if you have to convince highly people-attached colleagues about the merits of a new product, there's little chance that you'll win the argument solely by talking about the technical specs. Behavioural effectiveness depends on being effective with respect to your goals – either working alone or by engaging with others. Remember the 'Ten Commandments' from Chapter 3 (being on time, getting things done, being responsive, showing appreciation, etc.)? Well, in this first phase of working life, obeying the Ten Commandments is a large part of your behavioural effectiveness. Think of doing your research, submitting work of sufficient quality, hitting deadlines and all the rest, as the groundwork on which you'll build your future. As you progress, you'll realise that behavioural effectiveness means much more than following the Ten Commandments, but at this stage they'll help you substantially.

It's also through behavioural tools that your personal talent and natural preference come into play. If your AEM Cube profile revealed low people attachment, you're not likely to be successful in sales. If you scored highly on stability, opening a new office in another country is probably not a suitable assignment for you.

Our metaphor has its limitations. After all, learning how and when to use a hammer or screwdriver sounds easy enough, but it's not so obvious how to acquire workplace skills (unless perhaps you are literally a carpenter!). So, let's start with a real-life example. *A well-known CEO, who was a guest speaker at one of the authors' classes at the University of Amsterdam, told the students that he had learned his most important professional lessons from his first boss in a consulting firm. Every week, the boss would edit the trainee consultants' written advice to clients with a red pen. In the case of our guest CEO, the entire piece of paper turned red! But with every passing week, there was less and less red ink on his reports. Thanks to the boss, he was learning what good written advice looked like.*

Now let's look at another example. *When Sikko worked in executive search, he was involved in evaluating the management team of a medium-sized, family-owned company operating in a niche market. To the surprise of the owner who had requested the evaluation, the finance director was rated merely 'average', compared to finance directors Sikko knew in similar companies. But the owner thought the guy was fantastic 'because he always kept the accounts in order'. He'd never worked with a proactive finance director who helped take the business to the next level and had no idea what a 'good finance director' looked like. Instead, he was satisfied with someone who only had only assembled the toolbox of a bookkeeper.*

In short, to acquire good tools, you first have to know 'what good looks like'. With these two examples in mind, let's examine how to acquire the tools, as summed up in Exhibit 7.2.

Exhibit 7.2: Five ways to fill your toolbox

- The environment (structure, ways of doing things, level of people, professionalism)
- Education, courses (internal, external)
- People (craftspeople, professional, leader, entrepreneur, manager)
- Learning on the job (just do it)
- Trial and error

Discovering "what good looks like"

First, without any doubt, the environment you work in plays a key role. Here you become confronted with systems that are already in place, ways of doing things and levels of professionalism. You will not only see how to shape a marketing campaign, how to prepare an investment proposal or how to negotiate a procurement deal, but also how to organise cybersecurity and how to install a management development structure. Generally speaking, larger organisations (like multinationals and consultancy firms) know what good looks like in terms of systems and professionalism. But they may not know what good looks like in terms of entrepreneurship and agility. These attributes are more likely to be found in small- to medium-sized organisations. Different environments supply you with different tools.

Second, education and training can help you acquire further tools. There is a wide range of work-related courses to choose from, both from a content and behavioural point of view, but the outcomes depend very much on the quality of the programme and the people who are teaching it. Every additional training course you do will add to your toolbox, but you also have to realise that the truly important takeaways and long-lasting lessons will be limited. Even when there is active roleplay or simulation of work situations, real-life learning tends to have more impact.

When you ask experienced professionals how they acquired most of their learning, the vast majority will cite our third way to acquire tools: 'From the people I've worked with'. Like the CEO from our example earlier, they'll usually go on to tell you about the bosses, mentors and occasionally peers who taught them the most. But it's not just about teaching; it's also about *modelling* how to do something. If you can see 'what good looks like' in the people around you, you can observe and experience how they do things and then mimic them. Whether you aspire to be a craftsperson, an entertainer, a professional or a leader, you can usually find someone to learn from, provided you choose the right environment. If you want to become an entrepreneur, join an entrepreneurial organisation. And if you want to become a finance director, find an organisation where the person in that role is actively helping to develop the organisation, not just checking the accounts.

The two last ways to acquire your tools, learning on the job and trial and error, are related. Just by *doing* a job, you will see very clearly what sort of challenges are most common and how to deal with them... or not. Sometimes you might succeed, sometimes you might fail, but — provided you have the right attitude — you will have learned something. In this respect, the disadvantage of a large organisation is that you might be too protected. You'll hardly ever be thrown in at the deep end. On the other hand, people who start out in smaller organisations might miss out on some strategic education or professionalism, but they will probably learn how to take risks, make decisions and get things done.

As you'll discover when you are in the midst of the tool-acquiring phase, you'll feel that you're doing a lot more than just filling an empty container. You will think that you're already building your house. As you progress, you'll realise that — at best — you were building a room in your house or a shed in the garden, but not the entire building. As a member of Generation Y or Z, you may want it all now. This is only natural, but in the long term, the best policy is to be aware that your key objective for this phase of your career is to fill your toolbox with skills, knowledge and understanding of your talents — both in terms of content and behaviour. If that sounds a bit dull, consider that you can fill your toolbox in many different ways and with many different tools. That should give you enough variety to keep you entertained.

Even if you welcome the idea of filling your toolbox during the first phase of your own career, you might object that a few exceptional people do build their career houses very early in life. Indeed, during his career in executive recruitment, Sikko did meet a couple of such exceptions. One joined an online retailer as employee #4 at the age of 27, grew rapidly with the company and became CEO in his early thirties. He achieved organisational effectiveness very early, but only by virtue of growing with the business. In other words, he was still upgrading his toolbox at the same time as completing and even extending his house.

Another apparent exception joined the Executive Board of a Dutch retail chain at the age of 36, after a meteoric rise at a consumer multinational. He was able to secure the new role and succeed in it because his outstanding analytical skills prevailed over his less developed behavioural abilities. However, he too continued to improve his people skills over time.

It's interesting to consider how the attachment axis of the AEM-Cube, i.e., matter attachment (content) versus people attachment (behaviour) corresponds with this first phase in working life. Remember, very few people are positioned right in the middle of the axis. There is nearly always a preference for one end or the other. Knowing where your personal preferences lie helps you to better understand the kind of environment or role you will naturally excel in and, conversely, where you will have to put in more effort, as you continue to fill your toolbox. Exceptional circumstances or exceptionally sharp tools of one particular type may enable you to advance to the next phase(s) early, but you should still work on developing your fundamental skill set in order to build a solid house and live happily within it.

PHASE 2: BUILDING YOUR HOUSE

Although there's no clear cut-off point, some time around your mid-thirties you will move into the second phase of your working life, where you'll be confronted with a whole new set of challenges. To stay within our metaphor, you'll need all kinds of different expertise to build your house – bricklaying, carpentry, roofing, glazing, plumbing and electrics to name just a few – and they all need to be organised and aligned. What do you do when the bricks don't arrive on time? What happens if the windows arrive cracked? Or if the roof isn't watertight on the date the carpets are due to be delivered? During this phase, it will become clearer whether you are naturally suited to being a skilled craftsperson or an organiser and supervisor. In other words, whether you are more inclined toward personal effectiveness – linked to levels 1 and 2 of the maturity of complexity in the AEM-cube, as you may recall – or organisational effectiveness – which corresponds to levels 3 and 4. Whatever your natural preference, the most important difference between this phase and the previous one is that your performance is not just about you but depends on cooperation with others to achieve the desired result. The issues are of a different kind now too. The carpentry may well be exquisite but if the wires aren't properly connected and the carpets smell of damp, you won't have built a very nice house.

During this phase you will continue to acquire knowledge and skills. You will go on gaining experience, in terms of both content and behaviour, but the major difference compared with the tool-acquiring stage is the level of your behavioural learning in combination with your, already acquired, hard skills and experience, i.e., mastering competencies.

Although it's a fashionable term these days, 'competencies' is just a blanket term for combinations of knowledge, skills, talents and personality traits. Whatever you call them, they've always been important and there are many of them: teamwork, organisation and negotiation, to name just a few. The relevance of any given competency depends very much on the role and environment you are working in. Nevertheless, based on Sikko's experience, there are a few competencies which are essential for almost everyone. Time for another example...

Many years ago, Sikko participated in a training session with colleagues from around the world. One of the exercises was a roleplay, in which Sikko was an executive search consultant who had successfully helped an organisation attract managers over previous years and now had to pitch for a new assignment. One of his colleagues was playing the HR director of the client organisation, and Sikko was given five minutes to present to her. Off he went, first briefly explaining the latest developments within his own firm and then asking how his previous recruits were doing in the client's company. The 'HR director' discussed them all very briefly. They were doing well, as was the company, thank you very much. Then, Sikko ran through his pitch for the new assignment, based on his fictional track record. He was very pleased with how it went. But, to his horror, he was told he'd failed! Why? The brief given to the colleague playing the HR director was that she herself wanted to leave and that was what she really wanted to discuss with Sikko. He'd been so obsessed with his brief, that he'd paid no attention to her personally. If only he had said the magic words, 'How are you?', she would have opened up (as per her own brief) and eventually given him the assignment (as well as a talented HR director to pitch to other organisations). The main lesson he took away was always to show an interest in the person on the other side of the table.

This specific example comes under the broader umbrella competency of 'engagement with others'. Some of the Ten Commandments also fall into this category, but there are many others: communicating, organising, aligning, motivating and interacting with others. Likeability is arguably another example. Being liked and/or respected can be a powerful differentiator. Sometimes, a project or a role is awarded to you based on who you are, but after a while you'll have to back this up with results!

Other commonly mentioned competencies are conceptual thinking, reliability, initiative and responsibility. Again, how far you master these will depend on the environment you're operating in and your natural preferences (as suggested by your AEM-Cube profile). For the purposes of this book and this chapter, we'd particularly like to emphasise two other competencies which are important in almost every working environment.

The first is determination (which also came into the Ten Commandments). In any activity, whether at home, work or play, you will be confronted with challenges and setbacks. That shouldn't be a surprise — it happens to everyone. The difference lies in how people deal with it. Developing the will to overcome setbacks, along with the creativity and perseverance to find solutions, is a key to career success.

The second of these two key competencies, taking charge, tends to be a bit neglected. Today, 'leadership' (in the sense of aligning and motivating people) is high on the agenda, but taking charge, that is acting as the situation requires, is equally important. The situation concerned could be anything from managing a crisis or restructuring a department to defining a new strategy or seizing a business opportunity. Taking charge isn't easy. When do you step in? How do you balance the conflicting interests? How do you weigh the risks against benefits and — perhaps most important of all — the time pressures against the need for more information? Sikko's personal experience is that 'good leaders' not only dare to decide, but more importantly, know *when* to decide. Remember the third axis of the AEM Cube, maturity in complexity? The higher you are on this axis, the easier it is for you to oversee the system in which you operate and know when to decide.

In fact, maturity in complexity tends to become much more important during Phase 2 of working life. At this stage in your career, it's not enough simply to get the right blend of content and behaviour (any more than it is to just follow the 'Ten Commandments'). You have to take another step up because you'll be dealing with the kind of complexity which involves and affects other people. When Sikko was assessing the potential of young and mid-career executives in his role as an executive searcher, he used the model shown in Exhibit 7.3 (which Egon Zehnder has kindly allowed us to reproduce).

Exhibit 7.3: The four key indicators of executive potential

Curiosity	?	Seeks out new experiences, ideas, knowledge. Proactively seeks feedback and changes behaviour in response to it
Insight	◉	Proactively gathers and makes sense of a vast range of information, discovering new insights that, when applied, transform past views or set new directions (creates vision)
Engagement	♥	Engages the emotions and logic of others to communicate a persuasive vision and connect individuals to the organization and the leader
Determination	▶▶	Keeps driving to achieve the vision (goals of substantial scope and difficulty) despite challenges. While continuing to look for disconfirming evidence

When you take a closer look at these indicators of potential, you'll immediately recognise engagement and determination from our discussion above. You may also spot that 'insight' is shorthand for content, i.e., knowledge and hard skills. The only indicator we haven't yet alluded to, but which is crucial to developing your potential, is **curiosity.**

You will not grow if you are not curious. It's as simple as that. You should always be open to new opportunities, receptive to new learning and prepared to leave your comfort zone (as defined by the base of the AEM-Cube). But be careful. It's not enough to ask for feedback, accept advice and say, 'Thank you so much for that, I'm really going to work at it.' You also have to *do* something with this advice, creating a constant and virtuous circle of taking in new things and making them your own. Depending on your natural preference (for 'exploration' in the language of the AEM-Cube), you may be lucky enough to have more innate curiosity than other people. But through learned behaviour, you can also work on your curiosity.

Now let's return to the distinction we mentioned earlier – between personal effectiveness and organisational effectiveness. Personal effectiveness is about making a direct, individual impact on the end-consumer. Quite often, this involves a unique skill or talent, as in the case of performers (comedians, musicians, DJs, actors, athletes, etc.) and technical experts (doctors, lawyers, carpenters, consultants, marketeers, researchers, etc.). Organisational effectiveness, on the other hand, is generally less dependent on specific expertise or talent, because it involves organising what needs to be done in an effective and efficient way. Managers who are organisationally effective are able to put the right systems, people and working structures in place. Their success depends on their impact on others, who are collectively or directly responsible for the end result.

However, we have to be careful about labelling roles as based on personal or organisational effectiveness. Not everyone leading an organisation is by definition organisationally effective. *Sikko knows the founder of a complex, innovative, specialised maritime business, who was very successful because of his personal impact on the vision of the business and its ability to take risks. He was a technical expert and an entrepreneur but not very good at engaging people. Despite being at the top of a large and intricate organisation, his natural preference was for personal rather than organisational effectiveness. He never ran the company as a traditional top-down leader, working through heads of divisions and departments. Instead, he had individual dealings with people at all levels in the organisation: he was the spider in the centre of the web.*

Other examples of personally effective leaders are the managing partners of professional service firms. The vast majority have been consultants, accountants or lawyers for a long time and have been awarded the leadership role because of their professional reputation. The world isn't black and white. If you dig a bit deeper in many organisations, you find roles at many levels that demand elements of both personal and organisational effectiveness. All the same, it will help you in your career if you can understand your own preference.

Regardless of your natural preference, we have tried to describe what sort of challenges you will be facing as you build your house – and how to respond in terms of competencies, potential and effectiveness. The well filled toolbox of Phase 1 will help but is by no means a guarantee that you'll be able to handle the ongoing ambiguity of Phase 2. You cannot satisfy everyone. It's difficult to balance tough negotiations with long-term relationships. And it's even harder to align with people whose opinions contrast with your own. Arguably, in today's polarised world, it's harder than ever before. And some hot topics are unavoidable in the office. Should you pay more for renewable energy? Should you adopt a rainbow lanyard? It might seem impossible to balance all this with your increased responsibility and complexity. The most important lesson in the house-building phase of your career is about judgement regarding your own potential, but also about how well you can handle the challenges you face.

Let's illustrate this with another metaphor. Imagine you are at the bottom of a giant barrel in the garden of the house you are building. During this phase you will be moving up from floundering in the barrel to holding on to the edge and eventually sitting on the edge of the barrel, that is, having oversight and being in control. When you get another more complex role, you will be in an even larger barrel. The process will repeat itself, but you will progress to sitting on the edge more quickly.

To summarise, during this second phase of your career, you should find out what sort of environment you like, what roles you are capable of, what is really important to you in your working life and how to balance all that with your personal life. Hopefully, by the end of this phase at, say, 45–50 years of age, when you also fully comprehend the implications of your AEM-Cube profile in relation to the working world, you will have a far better understanding of where you fit in the job market. More than that, you should also be able to admit it. Knowing and accepting who you are will be key to your success and happiness in the final phase of your working life.

PHASE 3: LIVING IN YOUR HOUSE

By the time you reach this stage of your career, you should have realised what type of house is most suited for you. If you conclude that you are most comfortable in a semi-detached house, you should not strive for a detached luxury villa or step down to a poky little terrace. Both situations will cost you energy, for different reasons. We're not implying that you can't 'move house' during this phase. On the contrary, you can move to another semi-detached house, maybe slightly larger, with more bedrooms in a better location, but a move to that vast and sumptuous villa is less realistic.

In terms of your working life, this phase is likely to last some 15 years or more, during which you should still try to develop, but increasingly in environments and roles that align with your natural preferences. In this phase, it's essential to realise where you can add value and not to be too hung up about what others do or think. Recognition of your own merits should come from within and not by comparing yourself with others. If you wish, you can still make significant career moves with new challenges, whether in terms of personal or organisational effectiveness, but the essence of who you are and what you have become in relation to the working world will not change.

Let's return one more time to the previous two phases. We discovered the necessity of mastering content and behaviour in Phase 1, and added new factors such as curiosity, insight, engagement and determination in Phase 2. For Phase 3, all of these will remain important, but we'd like to add one more performance indicator: the ability to deliver. With any luck, you'll have had this ability for a while, but it's about to become crucial.

You may have heard the business proverb: 'A mediocre strategy with excellent execution is far better than an excellent strategy with mediocre execution.' In the end, that applies to individuals too. Whatever we do, we will largely be judged on the end result. Was your advice good? Did the parcel arrive as expected? Did the patient's condition improve after the operation?

If a product, service or outcome is not in line with expectations, personally effective people approach the situation in a very different way from organisationally effective people. Personally effective people take it into their own hands to ensure that expectations are matched, either by good planning or by putting in more hours. (That's not to say everyone who is capable of personal effectiveness lives up to their potential. We all know people who are sloppy, bad timekeepers or lazy communicators.)

For organisationally effective people, the solution is more complicated. They need to have resources and systems in place, especially when it comes to dealing with unforeseen circumstances, such as when third parties fail to deliver. Well-run organisations cater with such issues by managing expectations and having built-in provisions if things do go wrong.

WHAT THE AEM-CUBE MODEL TELLS US ABOUT DIFFERENT CAREER PHASES

We hope you have learned something from our characterisation of working life, but you may well be asking: how is this metaphor going to help me in my job choices? In order to join the dots between the three phases of working life and the types of jobs that go with it, we carried out a survey of 100-plus, early-, mid- and late-career professionals – in other words, people in the process of filling their toolbox, building their house and living in their house, respectively. The participants not only completed AEM-Cube personality tests but also, crucially, questionnaires that enabled us to position their current jobs on the same three dimensions (attachment, exploration and maturity in complexity). This enabled us to compare how personality, job profiles and the fit between them evolve over careers spanning decades.

We initially hypothesised that as people progressed through their careers, their job roles would gradually align with their personalities (as reflected in their AEM-Cube profiles) across the three career stages. However, our research didn't provide strong statistical evidence to confirm or refute this idea. What we *did* find was that, by the later stages of their careers, most people's jobs were reasonably well matched with their personalities. In other words, very few participants were working in roles that were significantly out of sync with who they were. This finding reinforced our faith in the AEM-Cube model!

We also found that young professionals in our sample group show a higher maturity in complexity than their jobs require. This pattern likely reflects more than just coincidence. Early in your career, it's common to concentrate on developing expertise in specific areas. Sometimes this is because you've chosen to 'build your toolbox', but often developing technical skills is something that comes with entry-level roles. This foundation later equips you to transition into more people-focused positions that are better aligned with your personality. The mismatch in maturity in complexity is also understandable – being entrusted with responsibilities that match your complexity in maturity takes knowledge and experience, even if your personal maturity in complexity after graduation qualifies you for more senior roles.

Another key finding came when we compared professionals at different career stages. Our data confirmed that people tend to grow in their ability to handle complexity over time. While early-career professionals from our sample were typically in specialist roles that did not require them to orchestrate people and inputs from various backgrounds and disciplines, late-stage professionals were more detached from the technical day-to-day workings of their organisations. This suggests that you can increase your maturity in complexity by seeking to understand the innate drivers of people with a different AEM-Cube profile from your own. The process is similar to the progression from personal to organisational effectiveness that we saw earlier in the chapter.

Does maturity in complexity automatically develop with age? While experience does help, there's more to the story. We found that people who are more exploratory are also better at managing complexity, in terms of both personal profile and job requirement (with a correlation of .23 and .30 respectively, for the statistics fans amongst you). Our most interesting finding was that, over time, exploratory individuals tend to develop a higher maturity in complexity and take on roles that require it. In fact, this was the strongest link in our research (with a correlation of .48).

We concluded that, regardless of age, taking on roles that require you to deal with novelty on a day-to-day basis helps you to rise swiftly to working on the 'big picture' of whatever activity you are in. The consequence for naturally exploratory people is that they should value this side of themselves and keep seeking roles, projects or organisational contexts that enable them to keep exploring, even in the final stages of their careers. Conversely, those who are more attracted to stability should continue to push themselves to leave their nice stable comfort zone, even after the early stages of their careers. How far you choose to venture outside that comfort zone will depend on your level of ambition.

AMBITION AND VALUES: THE ENGINE AND THE SHIELD FOR YOUR ENTIRE CAREER

The observant reader will have noticed that we haven't yet touched on the two horizontal bars of Exhibit 7.1 (at the beginning of this chapter): ambition and values. These are totally indispensable throughout your career journey because they are, respectively, the engine and shield of your potential, performance and effectiveness. Without these two ingredients, in balance, you have an insufficient frame of reference for exploiting your capabilities. But don't expect to have them both in equal measure for your entire working life. Neither will remain stable. Indeed, they will both change over time, in line with the three phases.

Let's look first at ambition. In some cultures, the word 'ambition' can have negative connotations. Consider comments like 'he has a big ego' or 'she only thinks about herself'. In other cultures, ambition is a sign that you're willing to invest in yourself and progress. However it's perceived, your level of ambition will be an important factor throughout your working life. There is no right or wrong, but having less ambition might hamper you in your personal development, in getting certain promotions or in getting a pay rise. Conversely, having too much ambition might alienate you from your colleagues and put you in situations where you are too far out of your depth to do a good job.

If at some point you decide that life outside work is what matters most and that you can make ends meet, that's perfectly fine. Provided it's your choice, you can accept the consequences and change the level or shape of your ambition. The decision could be based not only on your own work/life balance but also on a wide range of factors such as your partner's career or your parents' health.

In the early stages of your career, it may be difficult, if not impossible, to predict how ambitious you are. Some ambitions will be pretty clear. Most people want to become financially independent in some way, but others want to be the best in the class or become the boss. A few people might think they aren't ambitious when they clearly are! *In the course of his executive search work Sikko once spoke to a manager at an international airline, who said that he was not very ambitious. A perplexed Sikko asked why they were having a meeting in that case. He answered, 'I'm not sufficiently challenged, my job is too easy going and I miss being driven.'*

In short, your level of ambition is not necessarily fixed or obvious. It will change over time. As you progress you will get a better idea of 'how ambitious you are' at any given point. So don't worry too much about it at the beginning of your career. Just bear in mind that eventually your ambition will have an impact on your development.

Now to values. Are they the flipside of ambition? No, but some values may help you when your personal ambition and the organisation you work for are no longer aligned. Personal values (like commitment to your family or the planet) will help you keep your feet on the ground. But values are more than a curb on your ambition. The issue with personal values is not so much how to define them but how to balance them with your working environment. For personal reasons, you may not wish to be part of certain industries, such as tobacco, oil, arms or alcohol. Or you may not want to work for an organisation with a reputation as a polluter or exploiter of child labour (even if it has broken no laws in your own country).

Values can also be about the way you interact with people, e.g., sincerity, truthfulness and respect. There's not much debate about fundamental human values, but there are many cultural differences. In most Western cultures, personal and business values are pretty aligned. Lying, for instance, is bad at work, just as it is in life. In other cultures, not telling the truth may be accepted if it is in the interest of the business or out of financial need.

While you're filling your toolbox, the way you exercise your values is up to you. If you're not happy with the culture, don't join the organisation. If you're against ultra-processed food, don't apply to a big food manufacturer or a fast-food chain. If you want to stop hunger and malnutrition, you can join a charity or work in social policy instead. And if your value system comes into conflict with an organisation that you already work for, the outcome is again simple: you leave. The company may regret your departure, but it will probably have little influence on the business or on its other employees. There is, of course, another option: stay and try to change the culture. But in this first phase of your career, this is not necessarily realistic.

It's in Phases 2 and 3 of your career that integrating your values with your work becomes more challenging. These phases are characterised by greater complexity and greater responsibility, which means that conflicts of interest become more likely. As well as balancing your own value system with your work, you will have to navigate the needs of other people and sometimes *their* value systems. How can you balance climate goals with cost pressures, shareholder interests and employment security? If you withdraw from a geographical market because of human rights abuses, will it result in unemployment and even greater misery for the local people? Is the 'commission' you've been asked to pay in order to win a contract really a bribe? Regardless of the dilemma, it's unlikely that you can satisfy everyone. You will simply have to weigh the different interests, including your own, and use your judgement to find an imperfect solution. Hence our final piece of advice for building and living in your house: use every opportunity to develop your judgement in phases two and three of your career.

MEANWHILE, BACK IN THE PRESENT…

For now, however, let's leave the world of value dilemmas and return to the more pressing matter of your personal job-market dilemma. After all, you're probably not even in Phase 1 yet. All we suggest is that you take the learning from this chapter on board and factor it into your initial career choices. Don't stop there, though. While you are filling your toolbox in your first job, look around you at other people, who are already building their houses and living in them. Learn from them too – especially about how to develop and exercise judgement. Talking of which… you're now ready to make some difficult choices of your own! It's time to move on to Chapter 8, where we'll address the ultimate and most important question: how do I choose?

CHAPTER 8
HOW TO CHOOSE

At last, the chapter you have been waiting for! How is this book finally going to help you resolve your job-market dilemma? How will we bring your reasons for working, your self-awareness and your understanding of the working world with its three phases of working life together to support you in taking your career decisions?

When our students evaluated our classes at the Business School of the University of Amsterdam, our ratings were (very) good. Only one question resulted in a somewhat lower score: 'Do you have the tools to help you in your decision making?' When we delved deeper, it became clear that the students were expecting concrete answers about jobs, which they could start applying for straightaway.

Remon, the youngest of this book's co-authors, expressed his perspective as follows: 'My generation is very impatient; we want a quick fix for all the challenges we face as soon as possible, preferably yesterday.' The other two authors believe he may have been a bit unfair. Human beings of all generations like to have simple answers to complex questions. If you expect us to present you with concrete job titles to match your AEM Cube profile, this chapter may disappoint you. However, we promise to give you a process to follow and teach you how to use your newfound tools. Remember, as we saw in Chapter 7, tools on their own are not enough to build a house.

Through the examples we gave you in the previous chapters, we have tried to show you how important it is to have an open mind and not be too judgemental about career choices, whether orthodox or unorthodox. But having an open mind doesn't necessarily lead to a simple decision. The examples of Zack (our surfer friend from Chapter 1) and Yme (the booker-DJ from Chapters 1 and 3) show that they had an open mind but struggled to exercise it, mainly due to pressure, real or perceived, from their environment. When it comes to opening your mind, two things are important. One: unpeel your argument to the finest detail. Only then will you arrive at what you really want. Two: think through the consequences of the choice you are contemplating. Regardless of the outcome, in the end it is *your* choice, not your friends' or your parents' decision.

A BRIEF WORD ABOUT GENERATIONAL CHARACTERISTICS

Before we go any further, let's recap quickly on the lessons from Chapter 2 about generational differences. Are Generations Y or Z, with their distinctive characteristics, in a better or worse situation than their predecessors, in terms of their approach to and experience of the job market?

On the one hand, the Gen-Y-and-Z tendency to seek instant gratification gives you many different experiences to draw on and keeps you on your toes. On the other hand, gratification can't always be instant. We've heard examples of young professionals who were unhappy, because they did not get their boss's job within six months of starting work. Similarly, the generational desire to measure everything every minute of the day helps you to have confidence in what you are doing and where it's leading. However, if you're mainly measuring yourself against your peers, an unfavourable comparison can have a strongly negative psychological effect. And again, not everything you learn can be measured on a daily, weekly or even monthly basis. Knowledge and skills probably yes, behavioural learning less so. You need time to develop effective workplace behaviour.

There's one other element which is very important for your career development: perseverance and determination. That doesn't sit well with the generational preference to 'zap' between different movies and experiences or to 'scroll' rapidly through social media posts and activities. When you move on before finishing the last thing you were doing, does that indicate a lack of staying power? The easy answer is: 'Well, I do have determination and perseverance for things I *like* doing.' But at work there will inevitably be some stuff you don't like. After all, that's why people have to be paid to do jobs.

In short, if you share the typical characteristics of your generation, whether Y or Z, you will have to deal with them – like the generations that preceded you. The advantage you have over your predecessors is that we know much more about the differences between generations now. Unlike your elders, you will probably be able to recognise your generational advantages and disadvantages, which puts you in a much better position to exploit and overcome them respectively.

HOW SHOULD YOUR REASONS FOR WORKING INFLUENCE YOUR JOB SEARCH?

In Chapter 3 we analysed the seven main reasons for working. Each of the seven is valid, but it's difficult to take them all into account at the same time. Even more tricky, every reason for working has an impact on the others. For instance, if a high starting salary is important to you and you don't see yourself as an entrepreneur, the most logical options lie in sectors like consumer multinationals, financial services or consulting. But will these satisfy your desire to contribute to society? If a 'professional working environment' is high on your list, it's less likely that an NGO or start-up will meet your needs. But what about your passion for international development? The search engine in Exhibit 8.1 is a reminder that you will have to make trade-offs (a process that may frustrate your generational desire to 'want it all'!).

Exhibit 8.1: The search engine of reasons for working

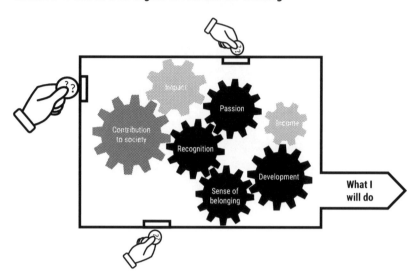

We believe that accepting the need to make trade-offs is essential for making a sound career choice, not least because it forces you to determine what, at this stage in your life, is really important to you. At the same time, making trade-offs prevents you from being naïve about the future consequences of your decisions. So how do you figure out what your true drivers for choosing your first job are? Our suggestion, especially if you have multiple ideas or options, is to make them all comparable.

Let's explain what we mean by using an example. Suppose you live in the capital of a European country, have a master's in marketing and a couple of years' experience. You are considering three options: one as a brand manager of a consumer corporate; one in a marketing consultancy firm; and the third as a search engine optimisation specialist at a new consumer start-up. The first pays €100K a year, the second €90K and the start-up €70K (we've rounded up for the sake of simplicity and future salary inflation!). The start-up is in the capital, the corporate is 40 minutes away by train and the consulting role is mainly abroad. The best way to compare them is to think in scenarios, for example, suppose all three are located in the capital and they all pay €70K. Or suppose they're all abroad and pay €90K. By approaching your options this way, you're forced to think about the content of the job and the working environment. Maybe the start-up has the most appealing job description, but the difference in pay is too significant for you not to take the corporate role. Through this hypothetical scenario, it has become clear that income is an important driver for you, which is perfectly fine.

Here's another example. Suppose you're torn between two job offers: one at a well-known brand, let's say Apple or BMW, and another at a totally unknown specialist tech or auto firm. In order to test how important brand recognition is for you, ask yourself how you would behave if you could tell your friends and family that the second job was in a different department of Apple or BMW? Which job would you take in that hypothetical scenario? Again, there's no shame in realising that recognition matters to you.

We covered 'passion' extensively in Chapter 3. The conclusion was that it's hard to define your passion and even harder to translate your passion into a working environment that you don't know. Worst of all, is the situation where you thought you knew your passion, and you later find out that it was the underlying factors that really mattered to you. Remember the basketball players in Chapter 3, who discovered that 'team sport' was their true passion and not basketball as such?

As you can see, passion remains difficult to deal with. Maybe it helps if we distinguish between people who truly *follow* their passion and those who are simply passionate about what they are doing. The first group is relatively small and mainly consists of 'performers' (in sports, music, etc.) or people with a particular interest and expertise in a certain subject (such as academics or writers). Their success depends very much on thriving in their environment. In fact, they often find it much harder to succeed in other environments. The second group is of a different kind. These people start their careers and become passionate about what they are doing as they go along. This is the vast majority of the passionately working population – and most of them are also able to get passionate about something else, which makes it easy to switch sectors, organisations and roles.

Let's now consider more examples of sporting passion, but from a different angle. Does the outside world recognise what's in the sportsperson's toolbox? Here's what two well-known Dutch sportspeople have to say about their own experiences. Esther Vergeer is a six-times Paralympic tennis champion and Pieter van den Hoogenband is a three-time Olympic swimming champion. Both were team managers ('*chefs de mission*') for the Netherlands at Paris 2024.

FROM SPORTING SUCCESS TO MANAGEMENT AND CONSULTANCY

Esther Vergeer made good use of advice and her fame in setting up her own foundation when she was still an active player. However...

It was exciting, also a bit scary, to be out of my comfort zone. My studies in management, economics and law did help in understanding things like finance and marketing but also in my roles of tournament director (ABN AMRO) and 'chef de mission'. The fact that these roles were given to me did help give me confidence and I also got a better understanding what 'working life' implies. Are all of my doubts now gone? No, so far, my 'sporting identity' did help me to get these roles, but will the outside world also recognise what I am capable of when it's something not sports related? I think I'll only know when I 'grow up'!

Pieter van den Hoogenband's father, Cees Rein, always told him: 'If you want to achieve something, you have to do your utmost.' But Cees Rein, who was a surgeon, had a medical career like his own in mind for his son! Pieter's swimming success convinced his father that following his passion was probably the right choice, but you can't swim yourself to financial independence. So, what was he to do after his sporting career?

A job at Eiffel (a consultancy) taught me a lot. The most important lesson is that, for the Olympic Games you work towards 'your peak', whilst elsewhere you have to perform all the time, reaching many small peaks.

The second thing is that, yes, the perseverance and discipline of my sports toolbox did help, but you have to be careful that you don't translate it one-to-one. Being in the pool at 6 o'clock is totally different from the discipline expected in communication with others: being responsive, thanking people for advice or hospitality, etc. A final piece of advice: do use your network and friends to get a better understanding of what is out there and, whatever that is, give it a fair chance by pulling your weight.

The moral of these stories is that – whether academic work, extracurricular activities, part-time work during your studies, your first job after university... or even Olympic success – you have to take some time and effort to reflect. Analyse your past experiences to understand your passions more fundamentally and identify the transferable skills or knowledge that you have already acquired from the activities you've truly enjoyed. We'll conclude our discussion of passion with a final example about passion from Sikko's career in executive search.

Sikko was searching for a managing director for a major professional football club, let's call it 'FC United'. His work was well underway, and he had a couple of good candidates lined up. Then he spoke to someone else who had an extremely relevant background for the position and was a diehard supporter of FC United. The new candidate couldn't wait to have a first interview. Sikko told him that he'd get back to him the next day.

After giving it some thought, Sikko came to the conclusion that the guy was too senior for the role. But how could he convince him? Time for a thought experiment! He phoned the candidate, as promised, and was immediately asked if the interview was all arranged. Instead of answering, Sikko told him that the firm had recently received a new recruiting assignment and, although he couldn't divulge the name of the organisation, the candidate's background was highly relevant for this post. The role was as follows: an MD position, a one-product company, one location, 100–150 people, turnover €50 million.

The candidate's immediate response was: 'I'm not interested. It's too small, not complex enough.' Sikko's response was: 'And if it's the MD role at FC United?' Only then did the football fan realise that he'd been carried away by his passion for the club. He hadn't looked at the facts of the role critically enough.

So much for passion; what about impact? As already mentioned earlier, just to strive to 'make an impact' is meaningless. First you have to unpack the spectrum of impact, just as you analysed your passion into its component parts. Do you want to make a direct individual impact through your work, within the organisation or externally? Or do you want to contribute to making a bigger impact *through* the organisation you're contemplating joining? Either way, our advice is to 'park' your desire to make an impact during the toolbox-building phase of your career, but to keep thinking about it in the terms described above. Only time will tell what the best way is for you to make your wish for impact come true.

As we mentioned in Chapter 3, personal and professional development comes high on the reasons-for-working wish list, according to a range of surveys. We reckon that this is because developing yourself is not only a valid goal in itself but also, in due course, helps to satisfy other reasons, such as income, recognition and purpose.

In the end, our advice about your reasons for working is to keep things simple. Get some clarity on how much money matters to you and focus most of all on building a platform for personal and professional development. If you truly are passionate about something, whether an activity or a wider purpose, by all means throw it into the decision-making mix. Otherwise, settle for something you do not *dis*like, whether a sector, a type of organisation or your everyday role. As mentioned earlier, along the way you will find out.

CHANNELLING YOUR SELF-AWARENESS

Do you really need to do a test, such as the AEM-Cube, in order to gain greater self-awareness? And how much can a generic questionnaire really tell you about yourself? Our view is that a test can help, but it is not a necessity – and it has its limitations. The most important thing is that you recognise the importance of self-awareness and commit to getting to know yourself over time. Let's look at another example.

What was Viv going to do after studying organisational psychology? The link with human resources seemed obvious and logical. Viv joined the HR department of a strategy consultancy but soon concluded that the job was all about playing host to new consultants and was far from the heart of the business. Switching to an international executive search firm seemed a good choice. After all, decisions about people were core to the company, while the clients' different roles and environments would make use of concepts from organisational psychology. It turned out that this new career also revealed Viv's own natural preferences and strengths. Constantly thinking about other people's profiles and how they fit with roles and organisations has been a source of self-development. Today, by gaining work experience, Viv is successful and appreciated, but also has a better sense of where to move in the future – guided by a passion for people.

Self-awareness is about how well you know yourself, complemented possibly by a personality test but more importantly by gaining working experience. The better you get to know yourself in relation to the world of work, the better you will understand why you like or dislike certain roles and what you are good or less good at. Especially at the beginning of your career, it helps to do jobs that are to some extent *outside* your comfort zone. This will make you better equipped for jobs *inside* your comfort zone in the longer run. But don't take this advice to extremes. If a role seems a long, long way from your natural profile, it's probably best to avoid it. Don't volunteer to open a new office on the other side of the world if you're strongly matter-attached and stability-focused!

Just a final word on personality tests before we move on to the job market itself. If you've done these kinds of tests in the past, you may have had a very common experience. That is, you recognise yourself from a personal point of view, but you're still unable to translate your test results into the world of work. Let's take a classic example (which we also touched on earlier in the book). If you're socially able (or like Viv have technical expertise in human psychology), the advice is typically: 'You should consider HR.' In most instances, this is completely wrong, because many HR roles are administrative or technical in nature, involving legal knowledge, policy documents, procedural details and calculations about salaries and incentives. Meanwhile, people skills (or at least behavioural effectiveness) are of extreme importance in all kinds of roles, such as sales or operations management. A test can help, but always take the obvious career advice with a pinch of salt.

THE WORLD OF WORK: THE WHERE AND THE WHAT

In Chapter 5 we gave you an overview of different sectors, organisations and roles. The time has now come to narrow this big picture down to some concrete options.

The more specific your studies are or were, e.g., medicine, engineering or law, the easier it is to follow a set career path. The difficulty comes when you consider making a switch, i.e., you decide you don't want to be a doctor, engineer or lawyer. What do you do? We just have one simple piece of advice: have a cup of coffee with someone who has made the same move − or at least someone who works in the new field you're considering. Informal conversations are essential for taking any new career direction, whether early or late in life. Suppose you're contemplating the move from medicine to public health or some other government department. Well, don't just read about the differences between the ministries and what the roles involve. Get additional information by talking to people. And don't just talk to friends who have recently joined (or left). Reach out to those who have 5 to 10 years' working experience. They will still be close enough to relate to but will be able to give you more of an overview. If networking doesn't come naturally to you, just think of it as research and remember that most people like talking about their careers.

What if you have a strong commitment to changing the world? Should you join an NGO? And if so, what can you expect? In almost any purpose-driven organisation you will find purpose-driven people. Yet, however like-minded they seem, purpose can come at the expense of professionalism and even common courtesy to colleagues. Even if you find a highly professional charity to work in, an environment that shares your purpose may not be enough if your day-to-day tasks aren't very interesting or the culture is difficult. And if your role lacks opportunities to develop yourself in preparation for your next move, whether internally or externally (to another non-profit organisation or a business), then the NGO really won't be a good idea. Let's look at another real-life example.

Lindsey studied marine policy in Miami, was passionate about nature and therefore joined an environmental NGO, working in Belize, the UK and Indonesia. Over time she has developed a specific expertise in the environmental conservation, fisheries and philanthropy sectors, and was asked by different NGOs and businesses for advice. Now Lindsey works mostly independently, serving several good courses as a consultant, having realised that there are more ways to do good for society than working for an NGO.

This example isn't entirely typical. In general terms, the not-for-profit and the business world have difficulties recognising what they can learn from each other and how skills developed in one can be used effectively in the other. Filling your toolbox in the housing or environmental department of the local municipality is by no means a guarantee that you'll be able to convince a construction or waste-management company of the usefulness of your tools in a business context. Such a move is only possible if you can develop specific expertise that is recognised and valued elsewhere (or if you have a personal contact). A move in the other direction is in principle easier. A not-for-profit organisation might well see the benefits of your business experience. However, they might also question whether someone with such a background can fit into their very different culture. Let's look at another example.

Nic studied international business and, despite wanting to make a contribution to society, decided to join a large consumer goods company, where there were many opportunities for professional development. Outside work, the new recruit continued to volunteer at charities for the less fortunate. Meanwhile, back in the office, Nic became involved in measuring the company's carbon footprint. After 15 years in sales and marketing for the same organisation, Nic finally decided to leave and start working for a company that specialised in the transition to electric transport. The new employer was looking for someone with broad sales and marketing expertise, although they did question whether someone with such a corporate background would fit into a much smaller organisation with a start-up culture. But so far, Nic's journey along the path to create meaningful impact is going smoothly.

One of the most common questions we're asked is: 'Should I join a large multinational or a smaller organisation? Maybe you're even tempted by one of the start-ups or 'scale-ups' that have emerged in recent decades as a result of digitalisation. Chris faced this choice around the age of 35.

For more than 10 years Chris had worked for a large international food retailer in commercial roles, before being approached to join the management team of a small sustainable fishing company. They knew each other because the retailer Chris worked for had always purchased canned fish from the smaller company. On paper, the move was crazy – from a large cash-rich professional organisation to a much smaller, less organised outfit with a totally different business model! But Chris decided to rise to the challenge of helping the fishing company to grow in a profitable way. Trying to get shelf space with large retailers worldwide proved difficult. Suddenly every euro counted towards a positive cash flow, and adding just one or two employees made the difference between profit and loss. But Chris is having a powerful learning experience in this 'housebuilding' career phase and has never regretted the change.

Start-ups, scale-ups and small companies can offer a very attractive package: entrepreneurial spirit, flexibility, informal and modern ways of working, and sometimes the possibility of a share in the ownership. All in all, it's often a stimulating environment. The flip side is that they're often less well organised, have less professional supporting systems and provide limited management development, at least in the sense of structured training. Another telling example is Arnie, who contemplated an early career switch.

At the time, Arnie was working for a large corporate employment agency and was asked by a group of friends to help set up a chain of food shops. It was a new retail concept, starting from scratch and entrepreneurial in spirit. After some serious thought, Arnie decided not to take the plunge. It seemed risky to work with friends, and the old job offered some exciting international experience. Though 'being entrepreneurial' was appealing, 'becoming an entrepreneur' felt like a step too far. Arnie eventually moved to a family-owned multinational with commercial and managerial roles in Germany, Thailand, the Czech Republic and Vietnam. Meanwhile, the start-up chain has over 10 branches and counting. It might have been exciting to be a successful entrepreneur, but Arnie's present job has brought rich international experiences of different cultures (national and organisational)... and some great entrepreneurial challenges!

This final example in the book shows that there is a big difference between working in an established company and joining a start-up or launching your own business, where the initiative is yours and yours alone. What should you consider before taking the plunge? Whether you've glimpsed a unique market opportunity or you've realised that you (and your potential co-founders) have a unique talent or skill that's in demand, remember that it makes sense to work with people whose abilities complement yours. Of course, this will need to happen if your venture is successful, but it's also more fun and more stimulating to work with complementary colleagues from the start. If you're in the early stage of your career, this will also given you a broader range of tools for building your career house. Apart from that, the main thing is to think things through carefully. You can never know if you'll be successful, but you can foresee what you might learn or what you might sacrifice if your start-up doesn't take off. If you've thought all possible scenarios through carefully — and you're still excited — then go for it!

At a large, household-name company, working life is relatively predictable. You know what to expect. The bigger the business, the more there is to learn from the general environment — whether professionalism, systems, knowledge or skills. In a smaller organisation, you can expect the unexpected! There will be learning from trial and error and a few special individuals. Most important of all you will learn to make things happen. If you are contemplating a smaller outfit, yes, look at the activity and maybe the business potential, but predominantly scrutinise the people, because 'knowing what good looks like' is the key to developing yourself, wherever you are.

Consulting is high on the list of many young professionals. Is it a good way to start a career or is it postponing your *real* job-market choice? And how can you give advice if you have little experience? There are, of course, many different consulting organisations, varying in size but also in specialisation and expertise. You will learn a lot in the larger consultancies in your first years: specific expertise (strategic, analytical, functional) and professional rigour. Plus, there is the fact that, by definition, you will work for a wide range of client organisations, which will multiply your knowledge of the working world and help you in your future choices. The vast majority of graduate or post-master's recruits leave consulting after 2 to 10 years. Only a few decide – or are invited – to stay and progress to managerial or partnership roles.

The mix of roles that follow consultancy is extraordinarily diverse. Some people go into specialist or expert roles, but others go on to become successful entrepreneurs, M&A advisers, private equity partners or eventually CEOs. The majority find that they have filled their toolbox well but are not necessarily well-prepared for building their house. Yes, they are personally effective, but that's not the same as organisational effectiveness – and there's no guarantee that their early consulting success will continue in a new context. The good news is that they have some great tools in their bag, and they've been exposed to people with managerial roles in many different contexts. They know 'what good looks like'. Now it's time to test their own ability to take charge. To sum up, consulting can be a great start to your career, but do realise that you will have less opportunity to lead people and take charge than in other environments.

Another common option is management traineeships. The more traditional corporates still have them. So, are they something you should consider? The good news is that they're more structured than they used to be many years ago. Rather than coming in, walking around different departments and looking over people's shoulders, you will be asked to do two or three different assignments over a two-year period. It can be a very good way to get to know a sector, organisation and culture, as well as to gain a better idea of what roles you'd prefer in the future.

So far, we have tackled the choice of environment rather than the choice of job, which in the end is equally important. If you are totally happy with your environment but not with the role, it won't last — and vice versa. There are so many different jobs and job titles that it's difficult to generalise, but it always makes sense to look not only at the title but also at the content of the job. Ask too how it relates to the Porter's model so that you can understand where the role fits into the bigger picture. However, especially at the start of your career, it's difficult to decide whether you should, for instance, strive for a more commercial or technical versus a more operational or organisation-wide support role. The truth is that there's likely to be a lot of trial and error, and the consequences of not finding a perfect fit in your first job aren't serious. 'Just do it' is, at the start, good advice. And while you're just doing it, keep an eye out for what other people are doing in their jobs. Maybe one of these roles would suit you better in the long run.

Sometimes you will know intuitively which role to take. When Sikko started working at a family-owned company, he was offered two roles: trading in tankers and financial controller. He opted for the second and learned that it was a bit too administrative for him. But he also learned that becoming a trader would have been a worse fit.

We realise that our very general advice about roles may not be to your satisfaction. Many readers will have hoped to find a direct link between their AEM-Cube profile and an ideal role. But first, there's no such thing as one perfect job to match your profile. Second, it's not such a bad thing to have an initial job that you don't entirely enjoy. And third, it's not us but *you* who should be taking the lead and the responsibility in this process. Nevertheless, let us help you along the road...

In our view, the best way of experiencing a role is by doing it. Of course, that's impossible if you don't even know if you want to get it! But there is a next best way of getting to know more about a role. And it's not reading the job description, trawling the website, studying the annual report or listening to the sales pitch of the recruiter. Instead, talk to people who are doing or have done a similar role. They will have no vested interest in selling it to you, but they'll almost always be happy to share their experience. As we said before, these cups of coffee are a necessity! In fact, they're an essential tool to add to your kit.

COMPETING WITH OTHER CANDIDATES: THE EMPLOYER'S POV

So far, this book has entirely focused on your view of the job market. It's been all about playing the game from your point of view. However, unless you start your own business (unrealistic for most people without experience), you'll be recruited by someone else on behalf of an organisation. The chances are that you're going to have to compete with others to get the job you want. And your rivals might win.

That's why we recommend considering several options at the same time. It's almost inevitable that you won't be able to coordinate all your applications with perfect timing, but with each application you make, you should be able to learn from the previous experiences. Whether you're offered the job or not, you should always ask *why*. We'll leave it to you to judge how appropriate it is to push for an answer, but in our experience, most rejected candidates are too quick to give up on getting to the truth (after all, not many people like receiving negative feedback). The recruiter will probably say something generic and non-committal like: 'Someone else was a closer match for the job description' (after all, not many people like giving negative feedback). But it would help *you* if you knew the real reason. So don't give up. Call the recruiter and ask a specific question: 'On a scale of 1 to 10, how would you rate me and the person you hired?' The difference in rating may not be very informative in itself, but it opens the door to the question 'What was it exactly that I lacked, compared to the successful candidate?' There may be many different reasons why you didn't get the job, but if a pattern begins to emerge after several rejections, you may need to rethink your choices.

It's important to try to see yourself from an employer's point of view. John F. Kennedy famously said, 'Ask not what your country can do for you – ask what you can do for your country.' In your case, 'Ask not what the organisation can do for you – ask what you can do for the organisation.' In our opinion there are two related ways of looking at this, one relating to the AEM-Cube axis of maturity in complexity and the other to a rule of thumb about who gives or takes.

As you rise through the four stages on the maturity-in-complexity axis, you progress from being solely responsible for your own work to being responsible for others' output. The higher you go, the greater the responsibilities you carry. In other words, there will be situations where you have to put the interests of the organisation and your colleagues over and above your own. That won't go on forever, but at times it will be necessary. In fact, these moments also occur at the beginning of your career. There will be instances, even in your first few months, when you ask whether you're giving a lot more to the organisation than you're taking from it, in terms of your modest salary and opportunities for development. You may even feel a bit exploited. This can indeed be the case but do try to see the company's perspective and the bigger picture before resigning! The situation may not be as simple as it seems, especially in terms of the value added by your job for the company and/ or the customer. It's very likely that the company is giving more value to you than you are creating for the company, but it can be difficult to see things that way at this precise moment.

Sikko's experience is that during the first tool-collecting phase of a career, the organisation creates roughly 75% of the value (measured in cash or otherwise) added by your job, while you bring just 25%. In the second or house-building phase, it's a more or less 50/50 share. And once you start living in your house, in the third career phase, you will add 75% of the value and the organisation 25%. This evolution should be reflected in your development and salary at each stage.

Suppose Sikko's rule of thumb is correct. Is it normal or right to move on to something else before you have started to give more and take less? The traditional advice was to stay in your early jobs for a couple of years, but if you are miserable, it may be better for you and the organisations concerned to cut your losses. After all, in the 21st century, changing jobs more frequently is the norm, and many employers are quick to shed staff when times get tough. There are always two sides to an argument, and such dilemmas don't have a single straightforward answer. All we hope is that our overall point makes sense: over time, it's important to find the right balance between your career path and the interests of the organisation(s) you work for.

SOME FINAL THOUGHTS BEFORE YOU PUT THIS BOOK DOWN

What are the key take-aways from this book for the reader? We hope you have gained:
- some interesting insights into the job-market dilemma;
- a different perspective on the job market by asking yourself the fundamental question about why you want to work;
- an appreciation of the importance of self-awareness;
- an overview of the working world, with its sectors, organisations and jobs;
- a basic idea about how your personality might match certain career options better than others;
- an understanding of the three phases of working life, including the difference between personally and organisationally effective people;
- some concrete tools and a methodology to help you search for your first or next job – and even to put in the bigger toolbox for building your 'career house'?

However, we foresee that your dilemma will not go away! On the contrary, in today's turbulent world, with its complex social pressures and heightened moral awareness, job-market choices are becoming even more difficult for Generations Y and Z. We would like to leave you with one final thought to help you deal with this mounting pressure effectively.

We've unashamedly borrowed that thought from Nobel Prize winner, Daniel Kahneman[13], a pioneer in the field of human decision making. In his book, *Thinking Fast and Slow*, he made the distinction between thinking in System 1, whereby the brain acts quickly, intuitively and without conscious effort and System 2, a slower analytical and more deliberate way of thinking.

The point we'd like to make is that, although job choices *should* be made carefully and deliberately in System 2, in practice, most people rely on the more intuitive approach of System 1. All we are asking from you is that you follow a more structured System 2 approach, based on the concepts of this book. If you do that, we believe you should be happy with the outcome, whatever that may be.

Part of this structured approach is, as we said earlier, to open your mind to unorthodox as well as orthodox choices. Don't get overly excited about an option or write it off, just because you think the people around you will have a certain opinion about it. That won't always be easy, but if you have looked at various options analytically by using this book, you will be able to explain your decision to yourself, your friends, your family, your teachers and/or your bosses.

You will also need to apply the same kind of thinking to your experiences once you start work. If you are unhappy in your job, take time to analyse *why* you aren't happy. As we mentioned before, peel off every layer of your dissatisfaction. Is it because of the people around you, your boss, the purpose of the organisation, its culture, its economic activity, the role itself... or something else? Also try to determine what you *do* like about it. Take all those reflections into account before you start looking for jobs elsewhere.

If you're still at university, whether at undergraduate or graduate level, we fully understand that you may not be ready to apply for a job right now.

But what you can do, is start working on the processes described in this book: the reasons for working, the self-awareness, the understanding of the working world, the alignment between personality and roles and the phases of working life. Finally, even if it's not time to choose yet, it's never too early to start learning how to choose. We'll leave you with Exhibit 8.2, a diagram you saw earlier in the book but may have overlooked at the time.

Exhibit 8.2: The missing link between you and the job market

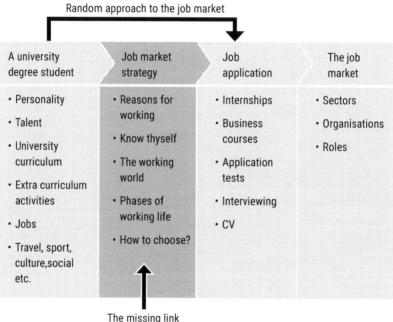

Start thinking, seek information and, most importantly, talk to people to obtain that information: your peers, your elders and others. Do that on (or well before) day one of your job search – and you'll find yourself far better prepared when you enter the crucial application and interview phase. If you remember one thing from this book, make it our final message: 'Don't be random. Be thorough and strategic!' Thinking slowly and methodically about why, how and where you want to work is the *only* way to successfully navigate your career through the turbulent waters of the job market.

ACKNOWLEDGEMENTS

As with many projects, our work has been shaped and enriched by the contributions of numerous individuals. We have been fortunate to engage in thoughtful discussions with many people who have come to us with their career dilemmas. Their perspectives helped sharpen our arguments, improve our work and inspire the development of this book.

First and foremost, we are deeply indebted to Folkert Mulder, who, from the very beginning, encouraged us to transform our ideas on addressing job-market dilemmas into a full course. His early support was instrumental in bringing this project to life.

We also extend our special thanks to the University of Amsterdam, and in particular to Marc Salomon and Mark van der Veen (Dean and Director of Education, respectively), for their trust and support in helping us integrate this course into the school curriculum. We are especially grateful to the hundreds of students we have worked with over the years. Their reactions, feedback and engagement not only made the process enjoyable but also provided us with invaluable insights that have greatly informed this work.

We are also deeply thankful to the more than 100 early-, mid- and late-career professionals who participated in our survey for this book, helping us connect the dots between the three phases of working life and the types of jobs that accompany them. We are sincerely grateful to each of you for your time and valuable insights.

Additionally, we would like to extend our heartfelt thanks to Sikko's former colleagues at the Egon Zehnder Amsterdam office for their valuable input and support, particularly in developing the sector overview. Their expertise and collaboration greatly enhanced the quality of our work.

A special thanks goes to Daniel Rebbin, our student assistant, who was initially retained to support the research but ended up contributing so much more. In addition to his hard work and enthusiasm, Daniel brought the critical perspective of our target audience. His dedication and insights were crucial to the success of this work.

We would also like to acknowledge the Human Insight team, stewards of the AEM-Cube, for their collaboration in refining our thinking and validating data. A special thanks to Peter Robertson, the creator of the AEM-Cube, for his vision, insights and generosity in allowing us to freely use and reference his work.

Our deepest thanks go to Elin Williams, who has been so much more than an editor throughout this process. Her ability to transform our ideas into clear, thoughtful prose was matched by her creativity, insight and dedication. Elin's constructive feedback and thoughtful contributions didn't just improve our work – they encouraged us to refine our thinking.

Finally, we are profoundly grateful to Anneke Zwanikken, Sikko's dedicated secretary for over 30 years. Her unwavering support, organisational expertise and tireless commitment in working through countless versions and iterations of chapters have been a cornerstone of this project.

While so many people have made valuable contributions to this book, any errors, misinterpretations or shortcomings remain entirely our own.

ABOUT THE AUTHORS

A unique three-generation, multi-perspective collaboration

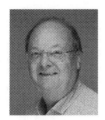 **Sikko Onnes** has seen the job-market dilemma from many different perspectives. First, back in the 1970s, as a graduate in business economics from the University of Rotterdam, he embarked on an international career in logistics and retailing with the family-owned company, SHV. During his second career, as a partner – for the executive search firm, Egon Zehnder, he came face to face with the job market in its bewildering breadth. Over the course of 30 years with the firm, he supported hundreds of people, as they wrestled with their own versions of the job-market dilemma.

As a father to three sons, now young professionals in their mid-thirties, Sikko realised that there were very few people capable of advising new graduates and young professionals on their first steps into the world of work. Most amateur advisors, usually parents and friends, have a limited grasp of the options – usually based on their own careers. Meanwhile, many recruiters have a vested interest and are not objective in their advice, and professional career advisors are not always available or too expensive for young graduates.

After retiring, Sikko started to fill that gap in the market with a well-regarded University of Amsterdam course, first for master's students and then for MBA participants. Now this course is transformed into a book.

Sikko is already the co-author of two publications. The first is about a special case of the job-market dilemma: that of top sportspeople preparing for a second career. The second is about summer houses on a small island in the northern Netherlands – an area of expertise that makes a surprise metaphorical appearance in Chapter 7!

Ron Soonieus may be the living embodiment of the job-market dilemma presented in his book. He studied international management and business administration at the University of Huddersfield and is now in his fifties... but still hasn't discovered what he wants to be when he grows up. Instead, he has built himself the ultimate portfolio career, covering a broad spectrum of the working world.

He started his career with a small, local Dutch firm. Very quickly realising this was not for him, he joined a large telecoms company, a tech company and then a bank, before building his portfolio career. Ron subsequently evolved into a strategy consultant and non-executive board member for a range of organisations. Today, his professional focus centres on the intersection of corporate strategy and corporate governance – topics on which he advises, teaches and writes. He is a Senior Advisor with Boston Consulting Group, a Director in Residence at INSEAD and serves on the board of the RADIX Think Tank for Business, Politics and Society, and the University of the Arts in the Netherlands.

Ron was using the AEM-Cube in his work when Sikko was looking to include a personality test in his course at the University of Amsterdam. Thus Ron got involved in developing the course with Sikko and eventually co-writing this book.

Remon Jasperse graduated just a few years ago – with dual master's degrees in business and economics from the Universities of Groningen (the Netherlands) and Fudan (China). He initially met Sikko when organising a careers event for fellow students, and the pair hit it off immediately. Sikko became a mentor in Remon's quest for a first job, and Remon, in turn, became a trusted sounding board for Sikko's ideas – a relationship that grew into a lasting friendship.

Remon is an enthusiast. His own dilemma was that he didn't know which of his passions to follow – whether to join a supply chain graduate programme, venture into strategy consulting or pursue a finance role. By applying the structured approach set out in this book, he was able to see the advantages, disadvantages and long-term implications of a whole range of options. Remon successfully secured his job in management consulting at KPMG Canada and, a few years in, feels confident he is on the right track.

He is now informally supporting his friends and colleagues with their own career dilemmas, passing on the learning and applying the structured approach that served him so well. In fact, it was he who initially pitched the idea of a book to Sikko and Ron. As Remon says, the ideas are so valuable that they deserve a much, much wider audience.

YOUR FREE AEM-CUBE TEST

Scanning the QR-code will direct you to the website of Human Insight. Here, you can fill out your name and email address to receive a free AEM-Cube report. You will receive the questionnaire in your inbox the next working day at the latest. Completing the questionnaire will take 8 to 12 minutes. After completion, you will receive your AEM-Cube report.

The AEM-Cube is a strategic assessment tool, developed by Human Insight, that identifies where people's natural strengths and talents lie, and how they can contribute to change and growth. It is based on 40 years of research and has helped more than 1.200 organisations. The tool offers unqiue insights into personal development, collaboration and career choices.

Human Insight is specialised in organisational and team development. The company also develops other strategic assessments, and researches organisational development and behavioural change.

Once you have your report, you will have the option of scheduling an online feedback session with one of Human Insight's coaches for a modest fee.

REFERENCES

1. Molinsky, A. (2019) '*The biggest hurdles recent graduates face entering the workforce.*' Harvard Business Review.
2. Brown, M. (2024) '*Study: Students lose confidence in career outlooks as they progress through college.*' LendEDU.
3. Johnson, W. (2019) '*Millennials and the quarter life crisis.*' LinkedIn.
4. Bradley University Online (2018) *Understanding the quarter-life crisis.*
5. Deloitte Global (2023) *The Deloitte Global 2023 Gen Z and Millennial Survey.*
6. Tapper, J. (2024) '*What's up with Generation Z?*' The Guardian.
7. Maslow, A.H. (1943) *A theory of human motivation.* New York: Harper.
8. Solnick, S.J. and Hemenway, D. (1998) '*Is more always better?: A survey on positional concerns*', *Journal of Economic Behavior & Organization*, 37(3), pp. 373-383.
9. Deloitte (2022) *The Deloitte Global 2022 Gen Z and Millennial Survey.*
10. RippleMatch (2022) *How Gen Z job seekers' priorities shifted during the pandemic.*
11. Robertson, P. P. (2005). *Always Change a Winning Team: Why reinvention and change are prerequisites for business success.* Singapore: Marshall Cavendish Business.
12. Porter, M.E. (1985) *Competitive advantage: Creating and sustaining superior performance.* New York: Free Press.
13. Kahneman, D. (2011) *Thinking, fast and slow.* New York: Farrar, Straus and Giroux.

Printed in the United States
by Baker & Taylor Publisher Services